墨香财经学术文库
"十二五"辽宁省重点图书出版规划项目
国家自然科学基金青年科学基金项目（71601033）研究成果

Generalized Container Loading Problem and Its Applications

广义集装箱装载问题及其应用

田甜 ◎ 著

东北财经大学出版社
Dongbei University of Finance & Economics Press
大连

图书在版编目（CIP）数据

广义集装箱装载问题及其应用=Generalized Container Loading Problem and Its Applications / 田甜著. —大连 : 东北财经大学出版社，2020.6
（墨香财经学术文库）
ISBN 978-7-5654-3725-0

Ⅰ. 广… Ⅱ. 田… Ⅲ. 集装箱-装载-研究 Ⅳ. U169.4

中国版本图书馆CIP数据核字（2019）第286884号

东北财经大学出版社出版发行
大连市黑石礁尖山街217号 邮政编码 116025
网 址：http：//www.dufep.cn
读者信箱：dufep @ dufe.edu.cn
大连永盛印业有限公司印刷

幅面尺寸：170mm×240mm 字数：144千字 印张：8.25 插页：1
2020年6月第1版 2020年6月第1次印刷
责任编辑：刘 佳 责任校对：徐 群
封面设计：冀贵收 版式设计：钟福建
定价：30.00元

教学支持 售后服务 联系电话：（0411）84710309

如有印装质量问题，请联系营销部：（0411）84710711

“东北财经大学‘双一流’建设项目
高水平学术专著出版资助计划”资助出版

作者简介

田甜，东北财经大学副教授，博士生导师。2014 年获香港城市大学商学院管理科学系博士学位。现任东北财经大学管理科学与工程学院院长助理、大数据管理与优化研究中心常务主任、大数据商务分析实验班项目主任，中国系统工程学会青年工作委员会委员。辽宁省“百千万人才工程”万人层次人才。在 *European Journal of Operational Research* 等国际期刊上发表多篇学术论文，主持国家自然科学基金青年项目 1 项，参与国家自然科学基金重点项目 1 项。

Preface

In the operations research literature, container loading problems are a class of geometric optimization problems in which three-dimensional items have to be loaded, entirely and without overlap, into large cubic spaces, such that one or more objectives are optimized. Many variants of container loading problems have been studied in the past several decades, but most of them are too simplified to describe a practical situation when loading containers.

In this book, we introduce the Generalized Container Loading Problem (GCLP) to model a more practical container loading issue. In this problem, we are given a set of three-dimensional containers and several sets of three-dimensional items. Each set of items can be further divided into two groups: mandatory items and optional items. Each container has a cost and each item has a value. We need to select one set of items and load all of its mandatory items, together with some or all of its optional items, into the container(s), such that the unit shipping cost is minimized. The unit shipping cost is defined as the quotient of the total cost of selected containers and the total value of loaded items. This problem successfully describes the multi-layer decision-making process and the trade-off between cost and value, which are common issues in logistics management.

Two applications of the generalized container loading problem are also demonstrated in this book, both of which represent real issues encountered by manufacturers in their logistics processes.

In the first application, an international audio equipment manufacturer would like to help its customers reduce unit shipping costs by adjusting order quantity according to product preference. We introduce the problem faced by the manufacturer as the Multiple Container Loading Problem with Preference (MCLPP). We prove that the MCLPP is a generalized container loading problem and propose a combinatorial formulation for the MCLPP. We develop a two-phase algorithm to solve the problem. In phase one, we estimate the most promising region of the solution space, based on performance statistics of the sub-problem solver. In phase two, we find a feasible solution in the promising region by solving a series of 3D orthogonal packing problems. We generate a large set of test instances based on the data provided by the manufacturer and conduct extensive computational experiments to demonstrate the effectiveness of our approach. A unique feature of our approach is that we estimate the average capability of the SCLP sub-routine in phase one and take it into account in the overall planning. To obtain a useful estimate, we randomly generate a large set of SCLP instances that are statistically similar to the manufacturer's historical order data.

The second application also comes from a manufacturer, whose products are stored in Palletized Storage Units (PSUs). PSUs are convenient for storage, but they are sometimes not cost effective for transportation because they can result in large empty spaces of waste in containers. To improve the utilization of its containers, the manufacturer is willing to remove products from PSUs (a process called depalletizing) and load the individual products, together with other PSUs, into containers. Once a PSU is depalletized, all of its products must be loaded into a container, such that all individual products can be rearranged into PSUs (a process called repalletizing) when the container arrives at its destination. Furthermore, no PSUs can be depalletized if the total volume of complete PSUs loaded in the container is not maximized. We introduce this problem as the Single Container Mix-Loading Problem (SCMLP). We prove that the SCMLP is a generalized container loading problem. Then, we develop a two-phase constructive algorithm for the SCMLP. This is based on a beam-search based method developed for loading items into a given set of spaces. In the first phase of our constructive algorithm, the beam search method is called upon to load PSUs into the container. In the second phase, a proper set of PSUs is selected (considering the remaining volume of the container), and the beam-search based method is used to load all products of the selected PSUs into the remaining spaces in the container. The performance of the constructive algorithm is demonstrated by experiments conducted on a set of instances generated from the historical data of the manufacturer.

This book is funded by "The 'Double First Class' Construction Project—High Level Academic Monographs" issued by Dongbei University of Finance and Economics. It is also supported by National Natural Science Foundation of China (Grant No. 71601033). I would like to express my deep gratitude.

Dr. Tian Tian
September 2019

Acknowledgements

Finishing this book was a journey full of challenges and hopes. I would like to express my greatest gratitude to all the people who have helped me to complete my book.

Foremost, I would like to express my sincere gratitude to my supervisor Prof. Andrew Lim for his continuous support and patience. This book could not have reached its present form without his encouragement and his trust.

I would particularly like to thank Dr. Yanzhi Li, Dr. Guangwu Liu, and Prof. Brian Rodrigues for their advices.

Next, I would like to express my gratitude to the other professors, teachers, and secretaries in the Department of Management Sciences of City University of Hong Kong and School of Management Science and Engineering of Dongbei University of Finance and Economics, who have helped me immeasurably over the past four years.

My deepest appreciation goes to my collaborators, Dr. Wenbin Zhu and Dr. Lijun Wei. They are excellent researchers who have provided valuable advice to me during the course of my research journey. I was always inspired by our heated discussions.

I want to express my heartfelt appreciation to my friends, who supported me in life and encouraged me to strive towards my goal. I also thank my labmates in City University of Hong Kong and colleagues in Dongbei University of Finance and Economics for their assistance and for the happy time we spent together.

Special thanks to my family. Words cannot express how grateful I am to my grandmother Mrs. Xianglan Wang and my mother Mrs. Hong Zhang for all the sacrifices they made on my behalf. Their understanding and encouragement have been what has sustained me so far.

Contents

1 Introduction / 1

1.1 Introduction / 1

1.2 Contributions / 4

1.3 Book Organization / 6

2 Literature Review / 7

2.1 Cutting and Packing Problems / 7

2.2 Typical Container Loading Problems / 8

2.3 Modeling Techniques / 11

2.4 Exact and Approximation Algorithms / 12

2.5 Heuristic Methods / 16

3 Generalized Container Loading Problem / 25

3.1 Introduction / 26

3.2 Problem Definition and Formulation / 27

3.3 Special Cases of the Generalized Container Loading Problems in Literature / 38

3.4 Conclusion / 41

4 The Multiple Container Loading Problem with Preference / 43

4.1 Introduction / 44

4.2 Problem Definition / 48

4.3 The MCLPP is a Generalized Container Loading Problem / 50

4.4 A Combinatorial Formulation / 52

4.5 A Two-Phase Heuristic / 55

4.6 Computational Experiments / 65

4.7 Conclusion / 78

5 The Single Container Mix-Loading Problem / 79

5.1 Introduction / 80

5.2 Problem Definition / 82

5.3 The SCMLP is a Generalized Container Loading Problem / 83

5.4 A Two-Phase Constructive Method / 85

5.5 Computational Experiments / 99

5.6 Conclusion / 103

6 Conclusion / 105

Bibliography / 109

Index / 117

1 Introduction

1.1 Introduction

A shipping container is a type of equipment utilized to carry or store goods, which was developed in 1956 by Malcom McLean. It replaced the traditional break bulk method of handling goods and facilitated the transportation revolution named containerization.

Containerization is a method of distributing goods in containers through an intermodal freight transport system. The intermodal transport system can be a combination of roadway, railway, waterway, airway, etc. In the system, containers are loaded, unloaded, stacked, and transferred from one vehicle to another (semi-trailer trucks, rail flatcars, container ships, cargo aircrafts, etc.) without being opened. Containerization dramatically reduced transportation costs by shortening shipping time, lessening the need for warehousing, and abating loss from damage and theft. By reducing transportation costs, containerization stimulated vast changes in where and how goods are manufactured and gave rise to the development of modern supply chains. Therefore, containerization supports international trade and is a major element of globalization.

Since 1956, shipment with containers has continued to be the preferred transportation mode for exporting and importing goods. Hence, problems arising in containerization have caught researchers' attention. Some of the problems involved in containerization are container loading problems, in which goods are loaded into containers to achieve some objective (e.g., minimum total cost of containers used to load all goods). Container loading is a pivotal function in containerization. Under-performance of container loading brings about unnecessary costs (e.g., cost of redundant containers) and unsatisfactory customer services (e.g., violation of deadlines). Therefore, it is not surprising that container loading problems have been studied frequently in operations research literature.

In literature, classic container loading problems include the single container loading problem, the three-dimensional bin packing problem, the three-dimensional variable-sized bin packing problem, and the multiple container loading cost minimization problem. Many solution methods have been developed for these container loading problems, ranging from simple constructive heuristics to advanced algorithms. However, most research-oriented container loading problems are too simplified to describe practical issues in the container loading process.

In this book, we introduce the Generalized Container Loading Problem (GCLP) to model a more practical container loading issue. In this problem, we are given a set of three-dimensional containers and several sets of three-dimensional items. Each set of items can be further divided into two groups: mandatory items and optional items. Each container has a cost and each item has a value. We need to select one set of items and load all of its mandatory items, together with some or all of its optional items, into the container(s), such that the unit shipping cost is minimized. The unit shipping cost is defined as the quotient of the total cost of selected containers and the total value of loaded items. This problem successfully describes the multi-layer decision-making process and the trade-off between cost and value, which are common issues in logistics management.

Two applications of the generalized container loading problem are also demonstrated in this book, both of which represent real issues encountered by manufacturers in their logistics processes.

In the first application, an international audio equipment manufacturer would like to help its customers reduce unit shipping cost by adjusting order quantity according to product preference. We introduce the problem faced by the manufacturer as the Multiple Container Loading Problem with Preference (MCLPP). We prove that the MCLPP is a generalized container loading problem and propose a combinatorial formulation for the MCLPP. We develop a two-phase algorithm to solve the problem. In phase one, we estimate the most promising region of the solution space, based on performance statistics of the sub-problem solver. In phase two, we find a feasible solution in the promising region by solving a series of 3D orthogonal packing problems. We generate a large set of test instances based on the data provided by the manufacturer and conduct extensive computational experiments to demonstrate the effectiveness of our approach. A unique feature of our approach is that we estimate the average capability of the SCLP sub-routine in phase one and take it into account in the overall planning. To obtain a useful estimate, we randomly generate a large set of SCLP instances that are statistically similar to the manufacturer's historical order data.

The second application also comes from a manufacturer, whose products are stored in Palletized Storage Units (PSUs). PSUs are convenient for storage, but they are sometimes not cost effective for transportation because they can result in large empty spaces of waste in containers. To improve the utilization of its containers, the manufacturer is willing to remove products from PSUs (a process called depalletizing) and load the individual products, together with other PSUs, into containers. It should be noted that, once a PSU is depalletized, all of its products must be loaded into a container, such that all individual products can be rearranged into PSUs (a process called repalletizing) when the container arrives at its destination. Furthermore, no PSU can be depalletized if the total volume of complete PSUs loaded in the container is not maximized. We introduce this problem as the Single Container Mix-Loading Problem (SCMLP). We prove that the SCMLP is a generalized container loading problem. Then, we develop a two-phase constructive algorithm for the SCMLP. This is based on a beam-search based method developed for loading items into a given set of spaces. In the first phase of our constructive algorithm, the beam-search method is called upon to load PSUs into the container. In the second phase, a proper set of PSUs is selected (considering the remaining volume of the container), and the beam-search based method is used to load all products of the selected PSUs into the remaining spaces in the container. The performance of the constructive algorithm is demonstrated by experiments conducted on a set of instances generated from the historical data of the manufacturer.

1.2 Contributions

We introduce the generalized container loading problem to model a new problem in container loading, and we study two applications of the generalized container loading problem. Our contributions are listed as follows:

1.2.1 The Generalized Container Loading Problem

(1) This is a new container loading problem, in which different sets of items are available, and each set of items is divided into the mandatory items and the optional items.

(2) This problem generalizes a large category of container loading

problems well-studied in the literature of cutting and packing problems.

(3) This problem successfully describes the multi - layer decision - making process in logistics management.

(4) This problem successfully describes the trade-off between cost and value in logistics management.

(5) Two mathematical models for this problem, which can be used for further research, are proposed.

1.2.2 The Multiple Container Loading Problem with Preference

(1) This problem is a practical container loading problem, in which user preference is considered.

(2) This problem is a generalized container loading problem, in which two sets of items are available.

(3) A new combinatorial optimization formulation is proposed for this problem, based on special relationships between item sets.

(4) We statistically estimate the impact of data characteristics on the performance of our sub-routine solver.

(5) An estimation of the performance of our sub - routine solver is utilized in the high-level planning of our heuristic.

(6) We demonstrate the effectiveness of our heuristic approach based on realistic test instances.

1.2.3 The Single Container Mix-Loading Problem

(1) This problem is a practical container loading problem, in which palletized stocking units can be depalletized.

(2) This problem is a generalized container loading problem, in which n sets of items are available (n is the number of palletized stocking units in each instance).

(3) A two-phase constructive algorithm is proposed, based on a beam

search based method that loads items into a given set of spaces.

(4) We demonstrate the effectiveness of our heuristic approach based on realistic test instances.

1.3 Book Organization

The rest of this book is organized as follows. In Chapter 2, we thoroughly review the literature on typical container loading problems, including the single container loading problem, the three-dimensional bin packing problem, the three-dimensional variable-sized bin packing problem, and the multiple container loading cost minimization problem. In Chapter 3, we introduce the generalized container loading problem and show how it generalizes the typical container loading problems. Then, in Chapter 4, we study the first application of the generalized container loading problem: the multiple container loading problem with preference. In Chapter 5, we study the second application of the generalized container loading problem: the single container mix-loading problem. Finally, in Chapter 6, we present a summary of this book.

2 Literature Review

The efficient loading of three-dimensional items into three-dimensional containers is a fundamental problem in the freight transportation and logistics industries. A great amount of literature in operations research has been devoted to various container loading problems, from single-container versions to multiple-container ones. In this chapter, we thoroughly review the literature on typical container loading problems, especially those written in English.

2.1 Cutting and Packing Problems

Most container loading problems belong to the category of cutting and packing (C&P) problems. In cutting and packing problems, two sets of elements are given and the elements can be defined in any shape and in one, two, three, or more dimensions. One set of the elements consists of big objects, each of which has a cost, while the other set consists of small items, each of which is associated with a value. The large objects usually correspond to cutting plates in cutting problems, and to containers or to the loading space of trucks and pallets in packing problems. We need to select some or all of the small items and big objects, such that all of the selected small items can be geometrically fitted into the selected big objects, such that one or more given objectives is satisfied. Here, geometrical fitness means that:

(1) all selected small items should be laid totally inside one of the selected big elements;

(2) all the small items that are assigned to the same big element do not overlap with each other.

The first thorough literature review of cutting and packing problems was done by Harald Dyckhoff and Ute Finke [19]. In their book, cutting problems and packing problems are categorized as a whole, and a consistent terminology for cutting and packing problems is proposed. Fifteen years later, Wascher et al. [86] proposed an improved typology for cutting and packing problems. They first generally divided cutting and packing problems into two types, namely input minimization problems and output maximization problems, based on different objectives. The objective of input minimization problems is to minimize the total cost of large objects that are selected to pack (or cut) all of the small items. In contrast, output maximization problems focus on ways to pack (or cut) the most valuable small items within a limited number of large objects. Then they further classified both input minimization problems and output maximization problems into seven intermediate problem types according to the basic characteristics of cutting and packing problems, including shape of small items, dimensionality of small items and large objects and assortment of small items and large objects.

2.2 Typical Container Loading Problems

Container loading problems are three-dimensional cutting and packing problems, in which small items of any possible shape are to be packed into large cuboid objects (or containers). The assortment of small items could be identical, weakly heterogeneous, or strongly heterogeneous, and the assortment of containers could be identical or weakly heterogenous. Some container loading problems can be categorized as input minimization problems, for example, the three-dimensional bin packing problem, while others are output maximization problems, for example, the single container loading problem.

In this section, we introduce some typical container loading problems that have received great attention from researchers. In the literature, it is common to define an item as feasibly loaded into a container if it is totally inside the container, its edges are parallel to those of the container, and it does not overlap other items in the same container.

2.2.1 The Single Container Loading Problem (SCLP)

Given a fairly large set of small cuboid items and one cuboid container, we have to pack some or all of the items feasibly into the given container, such that the total value of the packed items is maximized. The assortment of small items could be identical, weakly heterogeneous, or strongly heterogeneous. The SCLP is an output maximization problem, according to the typology developed by Wascher et al. [86]. If the volume of an item is viewed as its value, the objective of the single container loading problem becomes maximizing the total volume of the packed items. Single container loading problems can be further classified by the number of items of each type that can be packed into the container. If the number is limited with a lower bound and / or an upper bound, it is called a constrained problem; otherwise, it is an unconstrained problem.

2.2.2 The Three-Dimensional Bin Packing Problem (3DBPP)

Given a set of small cuboid items and an unlimited number of identical cuboid containers (or bins), we have to load all items into a minimum number of containers [79]. The assortment of small items is always weakly heterogeneous or strongly heterogeneous. The 3DBPP is an input minimization problem, according to the typology developed by Wascher et al. [86].

2.2.3 The Three - Dimensional Variable - Sized Bin Packing Problem (3DVSBPP)

It is different from the three - dimensional bin packing problem in that bins are of different dimensions, and thus the objective of the 3DVSBPP is to pack all small items into bins with minimum total volume or, equivalently, with minimum waste containers [9]. It is also an input minimization problem, according to the typology developed by Wascher et al. [86]. In literature, the 3DVSBPP is often refered to as the Multi-Container Loading Problem (MCLP).

2.2.4 The Multiple Container Loading Cost Minimization Problem (MCLCMP)

Given a set of small cuboid items and various cuboid containers with different dimensions and costs, we have to pack all items into containers, such that the total cost of used containers is minimized [11]. It is a variant of the three-dimensional variable-sized bin packing problem. If we set the cost of each container as its volume, then the MCLCMP is equivalent to the 3DVSBPP. The MCLCMP is an input minimization problem, according to the typology developed by Wascher et al. [86].

Research on container loading problems focuses mostly on modeling techniques, exact algorithms, approximation algorithms, and heuristic methods. Therefore, in the following sections, we briefly review literature on modeling techniques, exact and approximation algorithms, and heuristic methods of the typical container loading problems.

2.3 Modeling Techniques

Mathematical models help in better analyzing the solution space of a container loading problem. They provide information on optimal solution value, such as its lower and upper bounds, which is helpful for evaluating the quality of solutions found by the algorithms. The analysis of mathematical models is also the foundation of developing advanced solution methods, which are often combined with the branch and bound method, the branch and cut method, the column generation method, etc. In addition, mathematical models allow for the application of commercial solvers, such as LINGO and CPLEX, to solve container loading problems. Most mathematical models developed for typical container loading problems are integer or mixed-integer linear programming models.

Chen et al. [12] proposed a 0–1 mixed-integer linear programming model to capture the features of a series of container loading problems, including the three-dimensional bin packing problem, the three-dimensional variable-sized bin packing problem, and the multiple container loading cost minimization problem. It models the situations in which multiple containers are used and various types of small cuboid items are to be loaded. Specifically, the authors presented the item orientation and the weight distribution of items within each container as variables and constraints in their model.

Padberg [71] extended the mixed-integer formulation developed by Fasano [24] to model the single container loading problem. He also conducted polyhedral analysis on the model. The analysis shows that the linear programming relaxation of the model is a tighter approximation of the solution space of the problem than Fasano's model.

Junqueira et al. [49] also presented multiple mixed-integer linear programming models for the single container loading problem. Different from Padberg's model, their models take several practical constraints into consideration, including the vertical and horizontal stability of the small items within the container and the fragility of small items.

All of the above models clearly formulate the assignment of each small item to a container and its placement within the container, and, thus, they involve a polynomial number of variables and constraints. These models could be computationally inefficient, especially for large instances. However, both Chen's model and Junqueira's models prove that this kind of mixed-integer programming is useful because such models are easily modified to handle the special constraints of container loading problems.

Eley [21] proposed a set-covering model for container loading problems involving multiple containers, including the three-dimensional bin packing problem, the three-dimensional variable-sized bin packing problem, and the multiple container loading cost minimization problem. The author first introduced a concept called loading pattern, which refers to an arrangement of small cuboid items within a container. Each loading pattern has information on the type of container and the number of each type of item that is packed in the container. By introducing loading patterns, the author could hide the details of the assignment and placement of each item, making the set-covering model more compact. This model involves an exponential number of variables but it can be much more efficient than the other models, especially when the column generation method is used.

2.4 Exact and Approximation Algorithms

An exact algorithm is an algorithm that solves an optimization problem to optimality. NP-hard problems are optimization problems for which no polynomial time (or "fast") exact algorithm exists. Most container loading problems are strongly NP-hard combinatorial optimization problems because the one-dimensional bin packing problem, which is an NP-hard optimization problem, is their special case. Therefore, it is very difficult to solve container loading problems to optimality, even though there are efficient exact solution methods for the one-dimensional bin packing problem. The literature on exact algorithms for typical container loading problems is rather scarce, and we list some of the relevant studies as follows.

Martello et al. [58] developed branch-and-bound algorithms for both the single container loading problem and the three-dimensional bin packing problem. The branch-and-bound method may be the most popular technique used in exact algorithms. It consists of a systematic enumeration of all candidate solutions to the optimization problem. In the enumerating process, large subsets of candidate solutions are discarded because they are proven to be sub-optimal solutions. The lower bounds and/or upper bounds of the optimization problems are crucial in algorithms based on the branch-and-bound technique. Therefore, Martello et al. [58] introduced continuous lower bounds for both the single container loading problem and the three-dimensional bin packing problem. They proved the asymptotic worst-case performance ratio of the lower bounds to be 1/8. They also performed extensive computational experiments to test their algorithms and claimed that their exact algorithms could solve instances with up to 90 small items to optimality. However, only instances with up to 20 small items could be solved to optimality within a time limit. Martello et al. improved their branch-and-bound methods by fixing some flaws in [17, 59].

Hifi and Zissimopoulos [42] proposed two exact algorithms for a three-dimensional cutting problem, which is equivalent to the single container loading problem in the packing context. The first algorithm uses the dynamic programming technique, and it is extended from an approach designed for the two-dimensional version of the authors' cutting problem [35]. The second algorithm is also an adaptation of a method developed for the two-dimensional version of their problem [44], which is based on a graph search procedure with a depth-first search strategy. The two exact algorithms were tested to be efficient for instances with up to 50 items, although they could not find optimal solutions for all instances.

Most recently, Fekete et al. [30] developed a two-level tree search algorithm for solving high-dimensional packing problems, including various container loading problems, to optimality. They first invented a data structure for feasible packings based on graph-theoretic characterizations of interval graphs and then combined the data structure with other heuristics and the lower bounds they computed in earlier research works [25, 26, 27, 28]. They conducted computational experiments for instances with up to 80 small items, and more than 70% of these instances were solved to optimality. However, only instances with up to 20 small items could be solved to optimality within a given time limit.

The above literature shows that exact algorithms cannot solve container loading problems of practical sizes to optimality within a reasonable time limit. Therefore, researchers have tried to develop methods that can find sub-optimal solutions with proven quality and whose run-time bounds can be derived to be polynomial. These methods are called approximation algorithms [45, 85].

Hiff [41] proposed approximation algorithms for the unconstrained single container loading problem. One approximation algorithm is a four-stage algorithm extended from the author's previous work [43]. In the first three stages, arrangements of items, called x-stacks and y-stacks, are created and combined to produce feasible solutions. In the final stage, other feasible solutions are produced by solving single knapsack problems with the x-stacks and y-stacks produced in the previous stages. The best solution is selected from all feasible solutions found in the four stages. The author proved that the approximation ratio of this algorithm is at least 1/6, and the best homogeneous solution value could be obtained within $O(n)$ operations, where n is the number of small items.

Miyazawa and Wakabayashi [61] proposed an approximation algorithm, $A3S_m$ for a parametric three-dimensional bin packing problem. In the problem, all bins are unit cubes and all items have dimensions no larger than $1/m$, where $m > 2$.

Algorithm $A3S_m$ uses as a sub-routine the Hybrid 3D (H3D) algorithm [60], which is based on the hybrid first-fit strategy developed by Chung et al. [13]. The H3D algorithm first calls a three-dimensional strip packing solver to pack all small items into subdivided levels and then packs the levels into bins using a one-dimensional bin packing algorithm. The authors proved that the number of bins used by algorithm $A3S_m$ for a list of small items L is no larger than $\beta_m OPT(L)+70$, where β_m is a decreasing function of m and $OPT(L)$ is the optimal number of bins for item list L. Furthermore, algorithm $A3S_m$ can be implemented to run in polynomial time in terms of the number of small items.

Later, Miyazawa and Wakabayashi [64] developed an approximation algorithm for the three-dimensional variable-sized bin packing problem that allows item rotations. This algorithm combines the Hybrid 3D (H3D) algorithm [60] with a newly proposed algorithm, First Fit Decreasing Combine, which packs small items into columns. It can be implemented as a polynomial run-time algorithm and its asymptotic performance bound was proved to converge to a value smaller than 4.89.

In addition, asymptotic approximation algorithms for the three-dimensional strip packing problem were introduced by Li and Cheng [51, 52], Scheithauer [78], Bansal et al. [2], Jansen and Solis-Oba [47], and Miyazawa and Wakabayashi [62, 63, 61, 64]. In the three-dimensional strip packing problem, a list of items are packed into a column with a fixed-size bottom and an unbounded height, such that the height of the packing is minimized. The asymptotic performance bound of the approximation algorithm developed by Li and Cheng [51] is 3.25. About 20 years later, the bound was improved to 2.64 by Miyazawa and Wakabayashi [64]. Some authors also proposed approximation algorithms for special cases of the three-dimensional strip packing problem. For example, Li and Cheng [51] developed an algorithm for the special case in which all items have square bottoms.

2.5 Heuristic Methods

Heuristic algorithms have been developed for problems in which exact polynomial-time algorithms are known but are too expensive due to the input size. However, unlike approximation algorithms, heuristic methods usually only aim to find good solutions reasonably quickly, without a guarantee that the optimal solution will be found. Therefore, heuristic algorithms may be considered as approximate, but not accurate, algorithms. Sometimes, heuristicas algorithms can be accurate, that is, when they actually find the optimal solution, but such an algorithm is nonetheless called heuristic until its best solution is proven to be optimal.

According to El-Ghazali Taibi [82], "Heuristics find 'good' solutions on large-size problem instances. They allow to obtain acceptable performance at acceptable costs in a wide range of problems. They do not have an approximation guarantee on the obtained solutions. They are tailored and designed to solve a specific problem or/and instance..."

In the following sections, we briefly summarize the literature on heuristic methods for typical container loading problems.

2.5.1 Heuristics for the Single Container Loading Problem

Pisinger [75] classified the heuristic approaches for the single container loading problem into four groups: wall building approaches [7, 6, 33, 32, 34, 67, 73, 75], stack building approaches [31, 65], cuboid arrangement (or block building) approaches [8, 20, 22, 56, 89, 90], and guillotine cutting approaches [65]. This classification can be extended through the addition of horizontal-layer building approaches [4, 65, 76, 83].

In wall building approaches, the container is filled with walls (or vertical layers) of small items across one of its horizontal dimensions. George and Robinson [34] proposed the first wall building method for the single container loading problem. Several variants have been presented since then. Bischoff and Marriott [6] compared 14 different heuristics based on the George and Robinson framework.

Bischoff and Ratcliff [4] pointed out that wall building approaches might produce unstable packings, which is dangerous in transportation. They introduced a horizontal-layer building approach for the single container loading problem, in which the container is loaded from floor upwards using layers of up to two types of small items. This approach is an extension of the heuristic method proposed in [5].

After the development of the wall building and horizontal-layer building approaches, stack building approaches were proposed, in which the container is packed with stacks (or towers/columns) of small items. Gehring and Bortfeldt [31] developed a two-step stack building approach for the single container loading problem. In the first step, small items are stacked into towers, in which each item is fully supported from below by the surface of another item or by the container floor. Then, a genetic algorithm is called upon to arrange the towers into the container, thus solving a two-dimensional packing problem.

All of the above three types of building approaches simulate the process of workers packing items into a container manually.

The first cuboid arrangement (or block building) approach for the single container loading problem was proposed by Eley [20]. In this approach, the container is filled by cuboid arrangements (or blocks) made up of identical items. The author first developed a greedy search method to arrange the blocks and then improved the solution found by the greedy method using a tree search approach. Bortfeldt et al. [8] and Mack et al. [56] followed Eley's work by using blocks composed of identical items in their heuristic methods. Later, Fanslau and Bortfeldt [22] improved the performance of cuboid arrangement approaches by introducing blocks consisting of different types of items. Zhu et al. [90] and Zhang et al. [89] proved the efficiency of using both blocks of identical items and blocks of different items in heuristic methods for the single container loading problem.

Morabito and Arenales [65] proposed the guillotine cutting approach for the single container loading problem. In their approach, the container is partitioned by guillotine cuts into small parts in which only one item can be packed. The result of partitioning the container is called a "guillotine partition pattern", and each guillotine partition pattern can be represented in an AND/OR graph. The best guillotine partition pattern (corresponding to the best solution to the SCLP) can be found by determining the most valuable complete path in the AND/OR graph.

Different from all the above approaches, Ngoi et al. [69] developed an algorithm for the single container loading problem, which does not make use of any item arrangement (e.g., walls, stacks, etc.) and does not constrain the loading sequence (e.g., from back to front, from floor to ceiling, etc.). Their algorithm is based on a spatial representation technique proposed by Ngoi and Whybrew [68], in which the position and dimensions of each packed item and each empty space are stored in a three-dimensional matrix. The algorithm iteratively selects an item and places it in an empty space until stopping criteria are satisfied. Similarly, Huang and He [46, 40] proposed caving degree approaches for the single container loading problem, which do not make use of any special arrangement of items and do not constrain the loading sequence. They developed a placement rule based on the idea of caving degree, which always favors corners or even caves of the container when packing items, such that the items are packed as compactly as possible.

Lim et al. [53] also developed an approach for the single container loading problem, which does not involve any special arrangement of items but does stipulate that items should be packed from the floor up. In their Multi-Faced Buildup method, all walls of the container can be used as a base (or floor) on which to place items. Additionally, the authors combined the Multi-Faced Buildup technique with a look-ahead strategy to improve the solution quality.

Among all of the methods mentioned above, some are classic heuristic methods (e.g., the methods proposed in [4], [5], and [53]), while others are advanced heuristic methods (including tree search methods [20, 22, 75, 83, 89], graph search methods [65], the Simulated Annealing algorithms [56], the Tabu Search algorithms [8], the Genetic Algorithms [7, 31, 32], and the Greedy Randomized Adaptive Search Procedures [67, 73]). Commonly, classic heuristic methods are used to construct initial solution(s) for local search methods, such as, the Simulated Annealing algorithms, the Tabu Search algorithms, and population-based heuristics (e.g., the Genetic Algorithms).

2.5.2 Heuristics for the Three-Dimensional Bin Packing Problem

The first constructive heuristics for the three-dimensional bin packing problem were proposed by Martello et al. [58]. One heuristic, called S-Pack, is based on the horizontal-layer building method. The other heuristic, called MPV-BS, fills bins one after another by solving a series of single container loading problems using the branch-and-bound algorithm presented by the authors in the same paper.

Lodi et al. [55] proposed a two-phase layer-building heuristic for the three-dimensional bin packing problem and used it as the subordinate inner heuristic of a Tabu Search framework developed by the same group of authors [54]. In the first phase of the heuristic, items with similar heights are packed in the same layer. In the second phase, layers are built by solving a two-dimensional packing problem, in which item bases are to be packed onto layer floors with the same size as the container floor.

Both Martello and Lodi developed heuristic methods based on the horizontal-layer building approach. There are also heuristic methods with no special arrangement of items (e.g., walls and layers): for instance, the MPV-BS proposed by Martello et al. [58]. One important issue of these heuristic approaches is to devise an efficient and accurate placement rule that defines the position at which an item should be placed in a bin. In the MPV-BS, the placement rule is defined as "placing items at corner points of a bin", where the corner points are the non-dominated locations of an existing packing.

Silva et al. [80] suggested a two-phase greedy search heuristic for the three-dimensional bin packing problem with a stability constraint. The first phase is a constructive heuristic, in which items are packed into bins without any special arrangement and the placement rule is that each item should be inserted into a position that will cause the least increase in unusable space. In the second phase, the stability constraint is evaluated.

Faroe et al. [23] proposed a Guided Local Search heuristic for the three-dimensional bin packing problem. They first derived an upper bound on the optimal number of bins using a greedy heuristic. Then, they called upon the Guided Local Search technique to iteratively tighten the upper bound until a given time limit is reached or the upper bound matches the lower bound proposed by Martello et al. [58]. In each iteration, the Guided Local Search method constructs a packing of items using the upper bound number of bins; then, if the packing is feasible the upper bound is decreased by one. The authors did not mention the placement rule in their paper.

Parreno et al. [72] proposed a Greedy Randomized Adaptive Search Procedure for the three-dimensional bin packing problem. In its constructive phase, a maximum-space-based placement rule is used [73], which states that an item or several identical items should be packed into the maximum space with the minimum distance to a corner of the bin. In the improvement phase, several new moves are combined with a Variable Neighborhood Descent structure [36]. The authors also developed some pre-processing techniques to reduce the dimensionality of the problem. These techniques are called upon before the constructive phase.

Crainic et al. [14] developed two constructive heuristics for the three-dimensional bin packing problem without considering any arrangement of items. One heuristic is extended from the first-fit decreasing heuristic (EP-FFD), and the other is derived from the best-fit decreasing heuristic (EP-BFD). The most important contribution of this work is that the authors proposed a new placement rule based on the concept of extreme point, which is an extension of the corner point. Later on, Crainic et al. [15] presented a Tabu Search method for the three-dimensional bin packing problem, in which each iteration consists of two levels: the first level discards one bin of the input solution, and the second level verifies the feasibility of the new solution based on the graph-theoretical characterization developed by Fekete and Schepers [27]. An initial solution is computed by applying the EP-FFD heuristic developed by the authors [14].

2.5.3 Heuristics for the Three-Dimensional Variable-Sized Bin Packing Problem

Xue and Lai [88] proposed the first wall-building heuristics for the three-dimensional variable-sized bin packing problem. In these heuristics, items are ordered and arranged into walls, and the walls are loaded into bins.

The authors devised heuristic rules for item placement, item ordering, and wall building and combined these rules to solve the problem.

Brunetta and Gregoire [9] developed a tree search algorithm for the three-dimensional variable-sized bin packing problem. There are three steps at each node of the search tree: first, items are grouped into patterns using an extension of the pallet-loading heuristic developed by Morabito and Morales [66]; second, the patterns are combined to fill bins; third, items not included in any pattern are packed into bins using an extension of the container-loading heuristic developed by Pisinger [74].

Takahara and Miyamoto [81] presented a genetic algorithm for the three-dimensional variable-sized bin packing problem. This genetic algorithm determines the sequence of items and the sequence of bins in each chromosome. It calls upon a constructive heuristic to determine the position of an item, according to the sequences of items and bins defined by each chromosome. Their constructive heuristic uses no special arrangement of items, and its placement rule involves placing items at corner points (or "breaches", in their paper).

Ceschia and Schaerf [10] proposed a local search method for the three-dimensional variable-sized bin packing problem with a multi-drop constraint. This local search method works in an indirect solution space, which consists of item sequences instead of the actual solutions to the 3DBPP. At each iteration of the local search method, a procedure called "loader" inserts items into bins using a deterministic heuristic, such that the multi-drop constraint is satisfied.

2.5.4 Heuristics for the Multiple Container Loading Cost Minimization Problem

The multiple container loading cost minimization problem was first studied by Eley [21], who developed a bottleneck assignment approach. The author proposed a set-covering model for the multiple container loading cost minimization problem and then tried to solve it using the column generation method. One important feature of this approach is that packing patterns (or columns) are generated in advance using a tree-search-based heuristic.

Che et al. [11] extended the set-covering model by adding a loading factor parameter α to exploit the excess capacity of the chosen containers. They performed a binary search on α in their algorithm. All of the extended set-covering formulations with different values of α were solved using the column generation method, which is similar to that in the bottleneck assignment approach. However, three fast heuristic strategies were developed for generating packing patterns. It is obvious that the quantity and quality of the pre-generated packing patterns have a great impact on the performance of the column generation method.

Zhu et al. [91] presented a prototype column generation strategy based on the model proposed by Che et al. [11]. In their strategy, prototype columns were generated, and they played a role similar to that as actual columns (i.e., feasible solutions to the pricing problem) in the column generation method. These prototypes were realized into feasible packing patterns using a hill-climbing single container loading algorithm (only when necessary).

Wei et al. [87] combined the prototype column generation strategy with a goal-driven approach to take advantage of the special structure of the solution space of the multiple container loading cost minimization problem. The goal-driven approach enhanced the performance of the search procedure. The authors also devised a post-improvement procedure to reduce the cost of feasible MCLCMP solutions by replacing existing containers with cheaper ones.

2.5.5 A Summary of Heuristic Methods

From the above literature review, it is evident that a large portion of the research on container loading problems has been on heuristic methods. In general, heuristic methods for container loading problems can be categorized into three types: constructive methods, local search methods, and evolutionary methods.

In constructive methods [4, 8, 14, 31, 55, 80], items are packed into containers in stages; thus, a feasible solution is only seen at the end of the algorithm.

In local search algorithms, an initial feasible solution will be generated first using some constructive method. Then, new solutions are generated iteratively by making changes to solutions found in previous iterations, with the expectation that the new solutions will be closer to the optimum. The algorithm runs until some stopping criteria are satisfied. Some local search methods are trapped at the local optimum, while others have mechanisms to escape. Common local search methods used for container loading problems include the hill-climbing search algorithm [36, 50], the Simulated Annealing algorithm [36, 48, 84], the Tabu Search algorithm ([37, 36]), and the Greedy Randomized Adaptive Search Procedure (also known as GRASP) ([36, 67]).

Evolutionary algorithms usually start from an initial population of solutions. Then, they iteratively generate new populations and replace the current population by selecting solutions from the current and the new populations. This process does not stop until some given stopping criteria are met. There are several famous evolutionary methods employed in solving container loading problems, including the Genetic Algorithm ([31, 36, 38]), the Ant Colony Optimization Algorithm [18, 36], and the Particle Swarm Optimization Algorithm [39, 70].

3 Generalized Container Loading Problem

In this chapter, we introduce the Generalized Container Loading Problem (GCLP) to model a more practical container loading issue. In this problem, we are given a set of three-dimensional containers and several sets of three-dimensional items. Each set of items can be further divided into two groups: mandatory items and optional items. Each container has a cost and each item has a value. We need to select one set of items and load all of its mandatory items, together with some or all of its optional items, into the container(s), such that the unit shipping cost is minimized. The unit shipping cost is defined as the quotient of the total cost of selected containers and the total value of loaded items. This problem successfully describes the multi-layer decision-making process and the trade-off between cost and value, which are common issues in logistics management.

3.1 Introduction

In the generalized container loading problem, we are given a set of three-dimensional containers and N sets of three-dimensional items. Each container is characterized by its dimensions and cost, while each item is characterized by its dimensions and value. A special characteristic of the generalized container loading problem is that each set of items can be further divided into two groups: mandatory items and optional items. When a set of items is to be loaded into containers, all of its mandatory items must be loaded while some or all of its optional items can be left out. Therefore, in the generalized container loading problem, we have two decisions to make regarding the items: first, which set of items should be loaded into containers, and second, which optional items from the selected set should be loaded together with the mandatory ones. The objective of the generalized container loading problem is to minimize the unit shipping cost, which is defined as the quotient of the total cost of selected containers and the total value of loaded items.

The generalized container loading problem is abstracted from the field of logistics. In the modern logistics industry, supply chains and fleet management are being changed by issues including cross-continental fleet flows, intermodal freight transportation, and green logistics. Researchers and practitioners have to refine their processes in order to adapt to the changes. The generalized container loading problem summarizes some common issues in the process of adaptation. It describes the multi-layer decision-making process in the modern container loading industry, and it models the trade-off between container cost and item value, which arises in all transportation settings but is constantly ignored in literature. The generalized container loading problem also takes limitations on container availability into account.

We define the generalized container loading problem in Section 3.2.1. Then in Section 3.2.2 and 3.2.3, we present two mixed-integer programming models for the generalized container loading problem. The first model is adapted from the general model proposed by Chen et al. [12]. It is based on item-to-container assignment decisions and requires a polynomial number of variables and constraints, which makes it computationally inefficient. However, it can be easily modified to handle special considerations of container loading problems in industry, including weight distribution and item orientation. The second model is based on the set-covering problem. In a departure from the assignment model, we hide the details of the assignment and placement of items by introducing feasible loading patterns. This is more concise way to describe the generalized container loading problem, and it emphasizes the multi-layer decisions regarding item and container selection. It could be much more efficient than the first formulation, even though it has an exponential number of variables.

The GCLP generalizes typical container loading problems in literature, including the Single Container Loading Problem (SCLP) [20, 31, 34, 65, 76, 90], the Three-Dimensional Bin Packing Problem (3DBPP) [14, 15, 23, 29, 55, 72], the Three-Dimensional Variable-Sized Bin Packing Problem (3DVSBPP) [9, 10, 81, 88], and the Multiple Container Loading Cost Minimization Problem (MCLCMP) [11, 21, 87, 91]. We prove that these problems are special cases of the generalized container loading problem in Section 3.3.

3.2 Problem Definition and Formulation

The generalized container loading problem considers a set of three-dimensional containers with different costs and several sets of three-dimensional items with different values. Each set of items can be further divided into two groups: mandatory items and optional items. We need to select one set of items and load all of its mandatory items, together with some or all of its optional items, into the container(s), such that the unit shipping cost is minimized. The unit shipping cost is defined as the quotient of the total cost of selected containers and the total value of loaded items. In this section, we formally describe the generalized container loading problem by introducing notations and the two models.

3.2.1 Problem Definition

The set of available three-dimensional containers is denoted as $\mathcal{J}$. Each container $j \in \mathcal{J}$ is characterized by its dimensions L_j, W_j and H_j and its cost C_j. L_j is its length, W_j is its width, and H_j is its height. Containers with the same dimensions and cost belong to the same type, and the set of all container types is denoted as $\mathcal{T}$. Naturally, the cardinality of set $\mathcal{T}$ is no larger than that of set $\mathcal{J}$. We define function $\delta(j) = t \in \mathcal{T}$ for any container $j \in \mathcal{J}$ to show that container j is of type t. Thus, the cost of a type $t \in \mathcal{T}$ container is $C_t = C_j$, where $\delta(j) = t$.

We also clearly define the availability of containers. Let LB_t and UB_t denote the minimum and maximum number of type t containers that can be selected. UB is used to denote the maximum number of containers of all types that can be selected. UB should be smaller than or equal to $\sum_{t \in \mathcal{T}} UB_t$.

Suppose we have K sets of three-dimensional items. Let $\mathfrak{I}_k$ denote the k-th set of items, $\forall k = 1, \ldots, K$. Each item $i \in \mathfrak{I}_k$ has the dimensions l_i, w_i and h_i and the value v_i. l_i is its length, w_i is its width, and h_i is its height. Any set of items $\mathfrak{I}_k$ can be divided into two subsets in this problem, so we use $\mathfrak{I}_k^M$ to denote the subset of mandatory items and $\mathfrak{I}_k^O = \mathfrak{I}_k \setminus \mathfrak{I}_k^M$ to denote the subset of optional items.

The **basic constraints** of the generalized container loading problem can be summarized as follows:

(1) If a set of items $\mathfrak{I}_k$ is selected, all items $i \in \mathfrak{I}_k^M$ must be loaded into

containers.

(2) The number of type $t \in \mathcal{T}$ containers to be used should be within the range $[LB_t, UB_t]$.

(3) The number of all used containers should be no larger than UB.

(4) The resulting loading plan should be geometrically feasible.

A loading plan tells us what items and containers are selected and how the items are loaded into the containers. We define a loading plan as feasible if and only if the following **loading constraints** are satisfied:

(1) Each used container must contain at least one item.

(2) Each loaded item must be fully contained by one and only one container.

(3) Each loaded item must be placed with its edges parallel to those of the container it is in.

(4) Any two items inside the same container do not overlap with each other.

(5) Every item must be placed in one of its allowed orientations. In reality, not all products can be freely rotated. For example, certain types of household appliances must be mounted vertically because certain sides are fragile.

The objective of the generalized container loading problem is minimizing the unit cost, which is defined as the quotient of the total cost of used containers and the total value of loaded items. This objective is adopted from real applications. If both the total cost and the total value are measured by monetary value, the objective is minimizing the portion of cost in profit which is similar to minimizing the input-output ratio.

The generalized container loading problem is not modeled as a multi-objective (i. e., minimizing total cost and maximizing total profit) optimization problem because the solutions of a multi-objective optimization problem are not straight forward for the decision-makers: the result of solving a multi-objective problem is often a frontier consisting of more than one candidate solutions that do not dominate each other, therefore, the decision-makers still have no idea which solution to choose.

Furthermore, our objective is not simply to minimize the difference between the total cost and the total value because, commonly, the unit of the container cost is different from that of the item value. For example, the cost of a container could be the amount of money paid to rent the container, while the value of an item could be its volume, weight, or priority. Thus, it is not appropriate to simply deduct the total value of items from the total cost of containers.

Due to basic constraints (2) and (3), there can be no feasible solution to the generalized container loading problem when we cannot find an item set whose mandatory items can be totally loaded into the available containers. To handle this issue, a dummy container is introduced into set $\mathcal{J}$. We suppose the dimensions of the dummy container to be:

$$L = \max_{k=1,\cdots,K}\left\{\max_{i\in\mathcal{I}_k^M} l_i \times |\mathcal{I}_k^M|\right\}$$

$$W = \max_{k=1,\cdots,K}\left\{\max_{i\in\mathcal{I}_k^M} w_i\right\}$$

$$H = \max_{k=1,\cdots,K}\left\{\max_{i\in\mathcal{I}_k^M} h_i\right\}$$

Thus, the dummy container will be able to load all mandatory items of any item set. We also set the cost of the dummy container to be much higher than the cost of any other container, such that the dummy container will not be used when feasible solutions exist.

3.2.2 A General Model for the Generalized Container Loading Problem

In this model, we assign items into containers, so we clearly define the position of a loaded item in a container, the orientation of the loaded item, and the positional relationship of two items in the same container. To avoid misunderstanding, we first make the following clarification:

(1) Let the longest dimension of an item (or container) be its length, the shortest dimension be its height, and the middle dimension be its width.

(2) Suppose all containers are placed in the (+++) octant of the three-dimensional Cartesian system.

(3) Suppose each container is placed with its length along the x-axis, its width along the y-axis, and its height along the z-axis, as shown in Figure 3.1.

(4) Suppose the front-left-bottom corner of a container is placed at the origin of the three-dimensional Cartesian system, as shown in Figure 3.1.

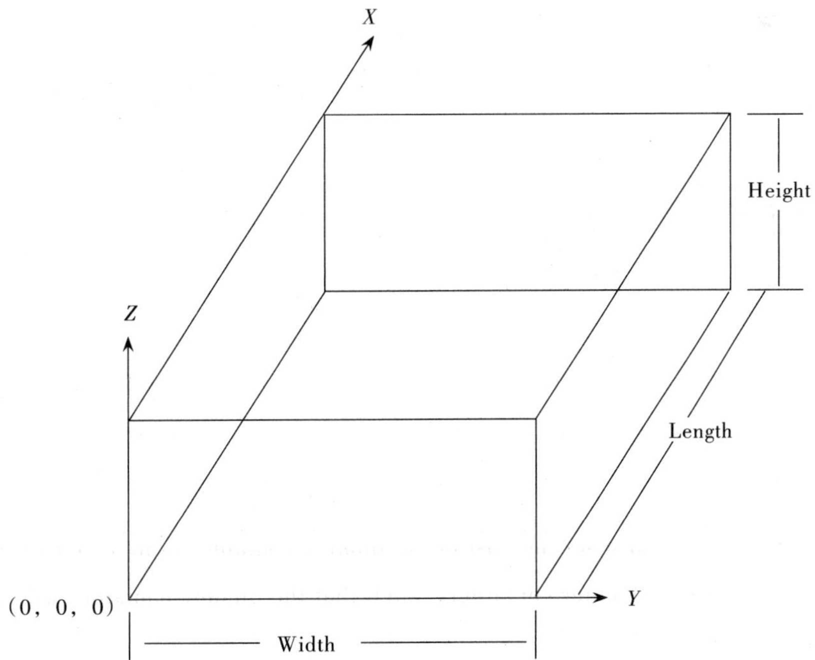

Figure 3.1 How a container is placed in the (+++) octant of the three-dimensional Cartesian system

Decision variables of the general model are listed as follows:

- Container selection binary variables α_j ($\forall j \in \mathcal{J}$): α_j equals 1 if container $j \in \mathcal{J}$ is used; otherwise, it equals 0.

- Item assignment binary variables β_{ij} ($\forall i \in \mathcal{I}_k, j \in \mathcal{J}$): β_{ij} is set to 1 if item $i \in \mathcal{I}_k$ is placed in container $j \in \mathcal{J}$; otherwise, it is set to 0.
- Item position continuous variables x_i, y_i, z_i ($\forall i \in \mathcal{I}_k$): the position of item $i \in \mathcal{I}_k$ is fixed by the coordinate of its front-left-bottom corner, which is (x_i, y_i, z_i).
- Item orientation binary variables ($\forall i \in \mathcal{I}_k$):
- p_{xi}, p_{yi}, and p_{zi} indicate whether the length of item $i \in \mathcal{I}_k$ is parallel to the x-, y-, or z-axis. For example, p_{zi} equals 1 if the length of item i is parallel to the z-axis; otherwise, it equals 0.
- q_{xi}, q_{yi}, and q_{zi} indicate whether the width of item $i \in \mathcal{I}_k$ is parallel to the x-, y-, or z-axis.
- r_{xi}, r_{yi}, and r_{zi} indicate whether the height of item $i \in \mathcal{I}_k$ is parallel to the x-, y-, or z-axis.
- Binary variables for the positional relationship of item $i \in \mathcal{I}_k$ and $i' \in \mathcal{I}_k$:
- $a_{ii'}$ is equal to 1 if item $i \in \mathcal{I}_k$ is in front of item $i' \in \mathcal{I}_k$; otherwise, it is equal to 0. Item i is in front of item i' if they are in the same container and $x_i < x_{i'}$.
- $b_{ii'}$ is equal to 1 if item $i \in \mathcal{I}_k$ is behind item $i' \in \mathcal{I}_k$; otherwise, it is equal to 0. Item i is behind item i' if they are in the same container and $x_i > x_{i'}$.
- $c_{ii'}$ is equal to 1 if item $i \in \mathcal{I}_k$ is on the left of item $i' \in \mathcal{I}_k$; otherwise, it is equal to 0. Item i is on the left of item i' if they are in the same container and $y_i < y_{i'}$.
- $d_{ii'}$ is equal to 1 if item $i \in \mathcal{I}_k$ is on the right of item $i' \in \mathcal{I}_k$; otherwise, it is equal to 0. Item i is on the right of item i' if they are in the same container and $y_i > y_{i'}$.
- $e_{ii'}$ is equal to 1 if item $i \in \mathcal{I}_k$ is below item $i' \in \mathcal{I}_k$; otherwise, it is equal to 0. Item i is below item i' if they are in the same container and $z_i < z_{i'}$.
- $f_{ii'}$ is equal to 1 if item $i \in \mathcal{I}_k$ is above item $i' \in \mathcal{I}_k$; otherwise, it is equal to 0. Item i is above item i' if they are in the same container and $z_i > z_{i'}$.

The interpretation of these variables is illustrated in Figure 3.2. There are two three-dimensional items loaded in the container: namely, item i and item i'. Item i is placed with its length along the y-axis, its width along the x-axis, and its height along the z-axis. Therefore, variables p_{yi}, q_{xi}, and r_{zi} should be equal to 1, while the other orientation variables should be equal to 0. Item i' is placed with its length along the z-axis, its width along the x-axis, and its height along the y-axis. Therefore, variables p_{zi}, q_{xi}, and r_{yi} should be equal to 1, while the other orientation variables should be equal to 0. In the case that item i is not loaded into any container, all the item orientation variables should be equal to 0.

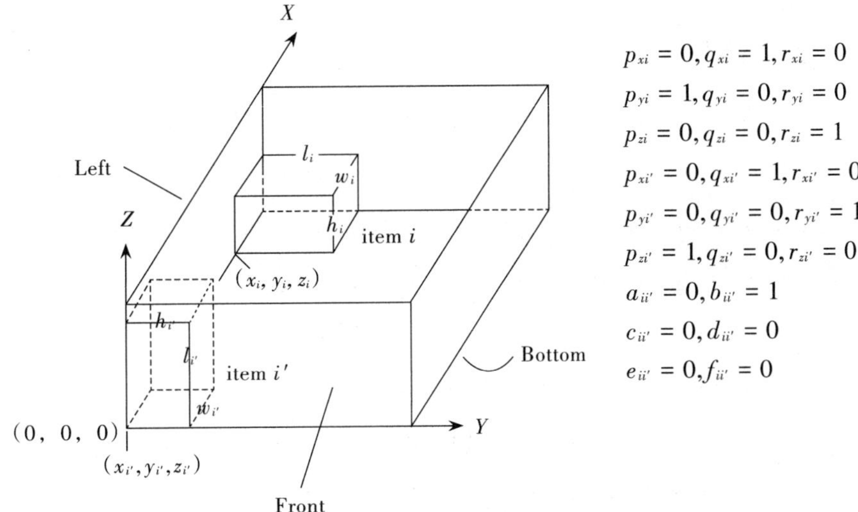

Figure 3.2 A demonstration of the variables of the general model

Figure 3.2 also shows that item i is behind item i', so variable $d_{ii'}$ should be equal to 1, while $c_{ii'}$ should be equal to 0. Since we have $y_i = y_{i'}$ and $z_i = z_{i'}$, all the other variables for the positional relationship of item i and item i' should be equal to 0. It should be pointed out that, if item $i \in \mathcal{J}_k$ and item $i' \in \mathcal{J}_k$ are in different containers, all binary variables for the positional relationship of item i and item i' should be 0.

Then, the generalized container loading problem can be modeled as:

$$\min_{k=1,\cdots,K} \frac{\sum_{j \in \mathcal{J}} C_j \cdot \alpha_j}{\sum_{j \in \mathcal{J}} \sum_{i \in \mathcal{I}_k} v_i \cdot \beta_{ij}} \tag{3.1}$$

subject to

$$\sum_{j \in \mathcal{J}} \beta_{ij} = 1, \forall i \in \mathcal{I}_k^M \tag{3.2}$$

$$\sum_{j \in \mathcal{J}} \beta_{ij} \leqslant 1, \forall i \in \mathcal{I}_k^O \tag{3.3}$$

$$\sum_{i \in \mathcal{I}} \beta_{ij} \leqslant M \cdot \alpha_j, \forall j \in \mathcal{J} \tag{3.4}$$

$$\sum_{j \in \mathcal{J}:\delta(j)=t} \alpha_j \leqslant UB_t, \forall t \in \mathcal{T} \tag{3.5}$$

$$\sum_{j \in \mathcal{J}:\delta(j)=t} \alpha_j \geqslant LB_t, \forall t \in \mathcal{T} \tag{3.6}$$

$$\sum_{j \in \mathcal{J}} \alpha_j \leqslant UB \tag{3.7}$$

$$x_i + l_i p_{xi} + w_i q_{xi} + h_i r_{xi} \leqslant L_j + (1 - \beta_{ij})M, \forall i \in \mathcal{I}_k, \forall j \in \mathcal{J} \tag{3.8}$$

$$y_i + l_i p_{yi} + w_i q_{yi} + h_i r_{yi} \leqslant W_j + (1 - \beta_{ij})M, \forall i \in \mathcal{I}_k, \forall j \in \mathcal{J} \tag{3.9}$$

$$z_i + l_i p_{zi} + w_i q_{zi} + h_i r_{zi} \leqslant H_j + (1 - \beta_{ij})M, \forall i \in \mathcal{I}_k, \forall j \in \mathcal{J} \tag{3.10}$$

$$x_i + l_i p_{xi} + w_i q_{xi} + h_i r_{xi} \leqslant x_{i'} + (1 - a_{ii'})M, \forall i, i' \in \mathcal{I}_k \tag{3.11}$$

$$x_{i'} + l_{i'} p_{xi'} + w_{i'} q_{xi'} + h_{i'} r_{xi'} \leqslant x_i + (1 - b_{ii'})M, \forall i, i' \in \mathcal{I}_k \tag{3.12}$$

$$y_i + l_i p_{yi} + w_i q_{yi} + h_i r_{yi} \leqslant y_{i'} + (1 - c_{ii'})M, \forall i, i' \in \mathcal{I}_k \tag{3.13}$$

$$y_{i'} + l_{i'} p_{yi'} + w_{i'} q_{yi'} + h_{i'} r_{yi'} \leqslant y_i + (1 - d_{ii'})M, \forall i, i' \in \mathcal{I}_k \tag{3.14}$$

$$z_i + l_i p_{zi} + w_i q_{zi} + h_i r_{zi} \leqslant z_{i'} + (1 - e_{ii'})M, \forall i, i' \in \mathcal{I}_k \tag{3.15}$$

$$z_{i'} + l_{i'} p_{zi'} + w_{i'} q_{zi'} + h_{i'} r_{zi'} \leqslant z_i + (1 - f_{ii'})M, \forall i, i' \in \mathcal{I}_k \tag{3.16}$$

$$p_{xi} + p_{yi} + p_{zi} = \sum_{j \in \mathcal{J}} \beta_{ij}, \forall i \in \mathcal{I}_k \tag{3.17}$$

$$q_{xi} + q_{yi} + q_{zi} = \sum_{j \in \mathcal{J}} \beta_{ij}, \forall i \in \mathcal{I}_k \tag{3.18}$$

$$r_{xi} + r_{yi} + r_{zi} = \sum_{j \in \mathcal{J}} \beta_{ij}, \forall i \in \mathcal{I}_k \tag{3.19}$$

$$p_{xi} + q_{xi} + r_{xi} = \sum_{j \in \mathcal{J}} \beta_{ij}, \forall i \in \mathcal{I}_k \tag{3.20}$$

$$p_{yi} + q_{yi} + r_{yi} = \sum_{j \in \mathcal{J}} \beta_{ij}, \forall i \in \mathcal{I}_k \tag{3.21}$$

$$p_{zi} + q_{zi} + r_{zi} = \sum_{j \in \mathcal{J}} \beta_{ij}, \forall i \in \mathcal{I}_k \quad (3.22)$$

$$\sum_{j \in \mathcal{J}} \beta_{ij} + \sum_{j \in \mathcal{J}} \beta_{i'j} - 1 \leqslant \theta_{ii'}, \forall i, i' \in \mathcal{I}_k \quad (3.23)$$

$$a_{ii'} + b_{ii'} \leqslant 1 + M(1 - \theta_{ii'}), \forall i, i' \in \mathcal{I}_k \quad (3.24)$$

$$c_{ii'} + d_{ii'} \leqslant 1 + M(1 - \theta_{ii'}), \forall i, i' \in \mathcal{I}_k \quad (3.25)$$

$$e_{ii'} + f_{ii'} \leqslant 1 + M(1 - \theta_{ii'}), \forall i, i' \in \mathcal{I}_k \quad (3.26)$$

$$a_{ii'} + b_{ii'} + c_{ii'} + d_{ii'} + e_{ii'} + f_{ii'} \geqslant \beta_{ij} + \beta_{i'j} - 1, \forall i, i' \in \mathcal{I}_k, \forall j \in \mathcal{J} \quad (3.27)$$

$$\beta_{ij} \in \{0, 1\}, \forall i \in \mathcal{I}_k, \forall j \in \mathcal{J} \quad (3.28)$$

$$\alpha_j \in \{0, 1\}, \forall j \in \mathcal{J} \quad (3.29)$$

$$p_{xi}, p_{yi}, p_{zi}, q_{xi}, q_{yi}, q_{zi}, r_{xi}, r_{yi}, r_{zi} \in \{0, 1\}, \forall i \in \mathcal{I}_k \quad (3.30)$$

$$a_{ii'}, b_{ii'}, c_{ii'}, d_{ii'}, e_{ii'}, f_{ii'} \in \{0, 1\}, \forall i, i' \in \mathcal{I}_k \quad (3.31)$$

$$x_i, y_i, z_i \geqslant 0, \quad i \in \mathcal{I}_k \quad (3.32)$$

M is an arbitrarily large number. The objective of this model is to minimize the unit shipping cost, which is defined as the result of dividing the total cost of selected containers by the total value of loaded items.

Constraint 3.2 ensures that each mandatory item of a selected set $\mathcal{I}_k$ is loaded into one and only one container. Constraint 3.3 makes it possible that some optional items of a selected set $\mathcal{I}_k$ are not loaded into any container and ensures that each selected optional item is loaded into one and only one container. If item i is placed in a container j, this container j is considered to be used. That is why Constraint 3.4 is included in this model.

Constraints 3.5 and 3.6 limit the maximum and minimum number of containers of each type $t \in \mathcal{T}$ that are available. Constraint 3.7 is used in cases in which the total number of containers that can be used is restricted.

Constraints 3.8 to 3.10 enforce that all items are totally placed within containers.

Constraints 3.11 to 3.16 ensure that the items in the same container do not geometrically overlap with one another. Take Constraint 3.11 as an example. If variable $a_{ii'}$ equals 1, the following constraints must be satisfied:

$$x_i + l_i p_{xi} + w_i q_{xi} + h_i r_{xi} \leqslant x_{i'}$$

This means that, when item i is in front of item i', there should be no overlap between the two items along the x-axis.

If item i is placed in a container j (i. e., $\sum_{j \in J} \beta_{ij} = 1$), the item orientation binary variables p_{xi}, p_{yi}, p_{zi}, q_{xi}, q_{yi}, q_{zi}, r_{xi}, r_{yi}, and r_{zi} should be carefully examined. In this case, the orientation variables are dependent, and they must satisfy Constraints 3.17 to 3.22. However, if item i is not loaded into any container (i.e., $\sum_{j \in J} \beta_{ij} = 0$), there is no need to consider the orientation of item i. In this case, we set p_{xi}, p_{yi}, p_{zi}, q_{xi}, q_{yi}, q_{zi}, r_{xi}, r_{yi}, and r_{zi} to be 0, which is also guaranteed by Constraints 3.17 to 3.22.

Constraints 3.23 to 3.26 are the linear expression of the following conditional constraints:

$$\textit{if} \sum_{j \in J} \beta_{ij} + \sum_{j \in J} \beta_{i'j} = 1$$

$$\textit{then}\ a_{ii'} + b_{ii'} \leqslant 1,\ c_{ii'} + d_{ii'} \leqslant 1,\ e_{ii'} + f_{ii'} \leqslant 1$$

These constraints make sure that if both item i and item i' are loaded into containers, item i will not be both in front of and behind, both on the right and left of, or both below and above item i'. If item i and item i' are in the same container, they must have positional relationships. This is guaranteed by Constraint 3.27.

We can replace five variables (p_{yi}, q_{xi}, q_{yi}, r_{xi}, r_{yi}) with the following formulations, such that the size of the model is significantly reduced.

$$p_{yi} = 1 - p_{xi} - p_{zi}$$

$$q_{xi} = p_{zi} - q_{yi} + r_{zi}$$

$$q_{zi} = 1 - p_{zi} - r_{zi}$$

$$r_{xi} = 1 - p_{xi} - p_{zi} + q_{yi} - r_{zi}$$

$$r_{yi} = p_{xi} + p_{zi} - q_{yi}$$

One contribution of this mixed-integer programming model is that it can be easily modified to handle special considerations of container loading problems in industry, including weight distribution and item orientation.

3.2.3 A Set-Covering Model for the Generalized Container Loading Problem

Before introducing the set-covering model for the generalized container loading problem, we need to define feasible loading patterns. A **feasible loading pattern** consists of a set of items and a container, under the condition that all of the items can be loaded into the container while satisfying all loading constraints described in Section 3.2.1. Suppose all feasible loading patterns, whose items are from item set $\mathcal{I}_k$, are stored in set $\mathcal{P}_k$. Since there are K sets of items in the generalized container loading problem, we will have K sets of feasible loading patterns.

Each feasible loading pattern must be associated with a container, so we define function $\sigma(p)=t$ to show that a container of type $t \in \mathcal{T}$ is used in pattern $p \in \mathcal{P}_k$. We use vector $\boldsymbol{a}_p$ to describe a feasible loading pattern whose elements a_p^i indicate whether item $i \in \mathcal{I}_k$ is placed in pattern $p \in \mathcal{P}_k$: a_p^i equals 1 if item i is placed in pattern p; otherwise, it equals 0. The cost of a pattern C_p is equal to the cost of the container, and the value of a pattern v_p is equal to the total value of the items in the pattern. Therefore, we have the following equations:

$$C_p = C_t,\ \forall p \in \mathcal{P}_k,\ \sigma(p)=t$$

$$v_p = \sum\nolimits_{i \in \mathcal{I}_k} v_i a_p^i,\ \forall p \in \mathcal{P}_k$$

Let x_p be the decision variables, such that x_p equals 1 when pattern $p \in \mathcal{P}_k$ is used; otherwise, it equals 0. The set-covering model of the generalized container loading problem is then stated like this:

$$\min_{k=1,\cdots,K} \sum_{p \in \mathcal{P}_k} \frac{C_p}{v_p} x_p \tag{3.33}$$

subject to

$$\sum_{p \in \mathcal{P}_k} a_p^i x_p = 1, \forall i \in \mathcal{I}_k^M \tag{3.34}$$

$$\sum_{p \in \mathcal{P}_k} a_p^i x_p \leqslant 1, \forall i \in \mathcal{I}_k^o \tag{3.35}$$

$$\sum_{p \in \mathcal{P}_k : \sigma(p) = t} x_p \leqslant UB_t, \forall t \in \mathcal{T} \tag{3.36}$$

$$\sum_{p \in \mathcal{P}_k : \sigma(p) = t} x_p \geqslant LB_t, \forall t \in \mathcal{T} \tag{3.37}$$

$$\sum_{p \in \mathcal{P}_k} x_p \leqslant UB \tag{3.38}$$

$$x_p \in \{0, 1\}, \forall p \in \mathcal{P} \tag{3.39}$$

The objective function 3.33 minimizes the unit shipping cost. Constraint 3.34 enforces that all mandatory items of set $\mathcal{I}_k$ are loaded into containers, while Constraint 3.35 ensures that some optional items of set $\mathcal{I}_k$ can be loaded into containers as well. The limitation on container availability is demonstrated by Constraints 3.36, 3.37 and 3.38, which have the same meaning as Constraints 3.5, 3.6 and 3.7, respectively, in the general model of the GCLP. The integrality of decision variables is guaranteed by Constraint 3.39.

Given this model, the only difficulty is that of generating all the feasible loading patterns for all item sets. Actually, the number of feasible loading patterns for each item set could be exponential and generating one feasible loading pattern could be equivalent to solving a single container loading problem, which is NP-hard. One possible method of solving this problem is heuristically generating a proper number of feasible loading patterns.

3.3 Special Cases of the Generalized Container Loading Problems in Literature

A number of classic container loading problems are special cases of the generalized container loading problem, including the single container loading problem, the three-dimensional bin packing problem, the three-dimensional variable-sized bin packing problem, and the multiple container loading cost minimization problem.

The single container loading problem can be modeled as a generalized container loading problem by considering that:

- Both $|\mathcal{J}|$ and $|\mathcal{T}|$ are equal to 1.
- The cost of the container is not significant: $C_j = 1, \forall j \in \mathcal{J}$.
- The limitation of container availability is defined as $UB_t = 1$, $LB_t = 1$, and $UB = 1$.
- There is only one set of items: $K = 1$.
- There is no mandatory item: $\mathcal{I}_k^M = \phi$, $\mathcal{I}_k^O = \mathcal{I}_k$.

The objective function of the generalized problem becomes minimizing the reciprocal of the total value of loaded items, or maximizing the total value of loaded items, which is exactly the objective of the single container loading problem. In most SCLP literature, the value of an item is represented by its volume. Then, the objective function becomes maximizing the total volume of loaded items.

The three-dimensional bin packing problem can be obtained by the following criteria:

- There is only one type of bin: $|\mathcal{T}| = 1$.
- All bins have the same dimensions: $L_j = L_{j'}$, $W_j = W_{j'}$, $H_j = H_{j'}$, $\forall j, j' \in \mathcal{J}$.
- The cost of each bin is not significant: $C_j = 1, \forall j \in \mathcal{J}$.
- There is no restriction on bin availability: $UB_t = \infty$, $LB_t = 0$, and $UB = \infty$.
- There is only one set of items: $K = 1$.
- All items of this set should be loaded into bins: $\mathcal{I}_k^M = \mathcal{I}_k$, $\mathcal{I}_k^O = \phi$.

Since all items should be loaded into bins, the total value of all loaded items is a constant. Moreover, the cost of each container equals 1. Hence, the objective function of the generalized problem becomes minimizing the number of used bins, which is exactly the objective of the three-dimensional bin packing problem.

The three-dimensional variable-sized bin packing problem can be obtained by considering that:

- The cost of each container equals its volume: $C_j = L_j W_j H_j$, $\forall j \in \mathcal{J}$.
- There is no restriction on container availability: $UB_t = \infty$, $LB_t = 0$, and $UB = \infty$.
- There is only one set of items: $K = 1$.
- All items of this set should be loaded into bins: $\mathcal{I}_k^M = \mathcal{I}_k$, $\mathcal{I}_k^O = \phi$.

Since all items should be loaded into bins, the total value of all loaded items is a constant. Then, the objective function of the generalized problem becomes minimizing the total cost of used containers. The cost of each container is defined as its volume, so the objective function of the generalized problem is to minimize the total volume of used containers, which is equivalent to the objective of the three-dimensional variable-sized bin packing problem. In most 3DVSBPP literature, an item's value is defined as its volume. In this case, the objective function of the 3DVSBPP is equivalent to minimizing wasted volume, which is the difference between the total volume of used containers and the total volume of all items.

The multiple container loading cost minimization problem can be modeled as a generalized container loading problem when:

- There is no restriction on container availability: $UB_t = \infty$, $LB_t = 0$, and $UB = \infty$.
- There is only one set of items: $K = 1$.
- All items of this set should be loaded into bins: $\mathcal{I}_k^M = \mathcal{I}_k$, $\mathcal{I}_k^O = \phi$.

Since all items should be loaded into bins, the total value of all loaded items is a constant. Then, the objective function of the generalized problem becomes minimizing the total cost of used containers, which is equivalent to the objective of the multiple container loading cost minimization problem.

3.4 Conclusion

In this chapter, we introduced the generalized container loading problem. In the generalized container loading problem, we are given a set of three-dimensional containers and several sets of three-dimensional items. Each set of items can be further divided into two groups: mandatory items and optional items. Each container is characterized by its dimensions and cost, while each item is characterized by its dimensions and value. We need to select one set of items and load some or no optional items, together with all the set's mandatory items, into the container(s), such that the unit shipping cost is minimized. The unit shipping cost is defined as the quotient of the total cost of the selected containers and the total value of the loaded items.

The generalized container loading problem describes some common issues in the modern freight transportation and logistics industry, which have not received enough attention in existing research. The contribution of the generalized container loading problem is two-fold. First, this problem describes a multilayer decision-making process, which is a difficulty frequently encountered by decision makers. The decisions include: (1) which set of items to choose; (2) which optional items of the selected item set should be loaded together with the mandatory ones; (3) which container combination should be used to accommodate all selected items. Second, this problem jointly considers container cost, item value, and practical constraints in container loading problems. In particular, the generalized container loading problem can handle different unit settings for container cost and item value.

We presented two mathematical models to capture the features of the generalized container loading problem. One is a mixed-integer programming model, which describes, in detail, the assignment and placement of items in containers. The other model is a set-covering model, which hides the loading details and dramatically increases computational efficiency.

A number of classic container loading problems were proved to be special cases of the generalized container loading problem, including the single container loading problem, the three-dimensional bin packing problem, the three-dimensional variable-sized bin packing problem, and the multiple container loading cost minimization problem.

4 The Multiple Container Loading Problem with Preference

An international audio equipment manufacturer would like to help its customers reduce unit shipping costs by adjusting order quantity according to product preference. We introduce the problem faced by the manufacturer as the Multiple Container Loading Problem with Preference (MCLPP). We prove that the MCLPP is a generalized container loading problem and propose a combinatorial formulation for the MCLPP. We develop a two-phase algorithm to solve the problem. In phase one, we estimate the most promising region of the solution space, based on performance statistics of the sub-problem solver. In phase two, we find a feasible solution in the promising region by solving a series of 3D orthogonal packing problems. We generate a large set of test instances based on the data provided by the manufacturer and conduct extensive computational experiments to demonstrate the effectiveness of our approach.

A unique feature of our approach is that we estimate the average capability of the SCLP sub-routine in phase one and take it into account in the overall planning. To obtain a useful estimate, we randomly generate a large set of SCLP instances that are statistically similar to the manufacturer's historical order data.

4.1 Introduction

Our team collaborates with an international audio equipment manufacturer to solve problems that had emerged in its logistics process. The manufacturer receives hundreds of purchase orders every day from all over the world. One of our tasks is to design loading plans for each purchase order, so as to minimize the per-dollar shipping cost. The per-dollar shipping cost is defined as the total shipping cost divided by the total dollar value of the items shipped. Minimizing the per-dollar shipping cost will reduce the unit cost and, thus, the sales price of the manufacturer's products, thereby improving its competitiveness in the market.

Currently, when fulfilling a purchase order, the manufacturer loads various items into containers in a sequential manner. As a result, all containers are almost fully utilized—except the last one. With regard to the last container, the manufacturer faces two common scenarios: either the container contains a small set of items, or it is quite full but still has room for several items. Slightly decreasing the order quantity in the first scenario and slightly increasing the order quantity in the second scenario will likely reduce the per-dollar shipping cost.

A discussion with the manufacturer's sales team reveals that recommending adjustments in order quantity is a viable option. Firstly, customers usually determine their order quantities based on forecasts, and forecasts are not accurate anyway. Therefore, most customers are willing to adjust their orders for sound reasons. Secondly, as mentioned above, reducing per-dollar shipping costs abates the unit cost of each product in the order, which allows the customers to increase their profits and their competitive advantage. Last, but not least, customers place orders regularly, and a slight change in a given order's quantity can always be compensated by an opposite change in the next order, if desired.

Consequently, the sales team would like to develop a decision support tool that will help their customers decide on the best order quantity to minimize their per-dollar shipping costs. The tool will be incorporated into the manufacturer's order-taking process and will work as follows.

Step 1. The sales team receive a purchase order from a customer and produces an initial loading plan using state-of-the-art multiple-container loading software. If the ordered items nicely utilize all containers, the sales team continues with the normal order-taking process (i. e., checking inventory, etc.).

Step 2. If one of the two scenarios for the last container occurs, the sales team runs our tool. The tool will slightly adjust the order quantity and produce an alternative loading plan so that the per-dollar shipping cost is reduced as much as possible. The sales team then sends back the adjusted order, together with the corresponding loading plan, and explains to the customer why the adjusted order is beneficial.

Step 3. The customer may stick to its original order, switch to the recommended order, or set certain restrictions and ask the sales team to adjust again. Once the customer decides on the order quantity, the sales team continues with the normal order-taking process.

For the decision support tool to be applicable, the adjustment must be easy to explain to the customers. A further discussion with the manufacturer sets the following criteria.

Unidirectional Adjustment: We can either increase or decrease the order quantity, but we cannot do both at the same time. Theoretically speaking, the loading plan with the minimum per-dollar shipping cost may be obtained by increasing the quantity of some products and decreasing the quantity of other products at the same time. However, such changes cause a large deviation from the original order and, thus, are hard to explain to customers. There is a danger of the alteration being misunderstood as a move to take advantage of customers for the purpose of inventory control. In contrast, it is much easier for the alteration to be accepted if the manufacturer says, "These few items require a separate container, and we recommend you to remove them to save shipping cost" or "The last container is almost full, but it has room for a few more items, so we recommend that you load more items."

No Piggyback: Products not in the original order will not be introduced into the adjusted order. The manufacturer produces many different products, and a customer usually orders a small subset of these products. It is very hard to predict which additional products the customer may like. Therefore, it is much safer to increase the quantity of existing products in the original order than to recommend new products that the customer may not like at all. This criterion is not as restrictive as it seems. For example, if a customer does not mind including additional products selected from a specific list, we can handle the situation by taking the list into consideration when adjusting the order quantity.

Bounded Quantity: The quantity of each product in the adjusted order must fall within a given range. There are three reasons for setting a bound on the adjustment of each product. Firstly, the inventory or production capacity sets an upper bound (although, for most products, we can safely ignore this). Secondly, customers rarely accept dramatic changes, such as doubling or halving the quantity of one product, though they are willing to consider milder changes. Thirdly, the sales team does not want to reduce the order quantity by too much, since this reduces profit. However, if a slight reduction in order quantity results in a noticeable reduction in per-dollar shipping cost, the manufacturer has an incentive to help the customer in an effort to maintain a long-term relationship.

Preference-Driven Adjustment: Order quantity should be increased or decreased according to product preferences. We expect our decision support tool to be useful in various practical situations, although its primary motivation is to minimize per-dollar shipping cost. For this purpose, we use preference instead of dollar value to evaluate each product and, thus, change the objective to minimizing shipping cost per unit preference, which is defined as the total shipping cost divided by the total preference of loaded products. There are a few indicators that may determine a product's preference, such as delivery deadline, shelf life, and dollar value. For instance, fashion products have shorter shelf lives than ordinary products, and we should make sure that fashion products are delivered as soon as possible. In this case, shelf life should be used as the preference indicator, and a high preference will be assigned to a fashion product. Furthermore, the preference of a product may be determined by different indicators in different situations. As an example, if only various fashion products are being delivered, dollar value may be used as the preference indicator instead of shelf life. In more complicated situations, several indicators may be combined to determine a product's preference.

To summarize, the manufacturer's sales team needs a tool that adjusts order quantity according to product preferences, while satisfying certain constraints, and that generates loading plans for the adjusted order so that the shipping cost per unit preference is minimized. We name the resulting optimization problem the Multiple Container Loading Problem with Preference (MCLPP), and it is formally defined in Section 4.2.

In Section 4.3, we prove that the MCLPP is a generalized container loading problem and determine a special property of the MCLPP. Then, in Section 4.4, we propose a combinatorial formulation for the MCLPP based on the concept of loading-plan sets. Each loading-plan set is a group of shipping plans with the same total cost and total preference. We further show that an optimal solution to the MCLPP must lie in one dominating loading-plan set.

Accordingly, a two-phase heuristic is developed for the MCLPP, as described in Section 4.5. In phase one, we try to quickly estimate the dominating loading-plan sets instead of invoking the time-consuming sub-problem solvers. The estimation is based on the performance statistics of sub-problem solvers on randomly generated MCLPP instances with similar characteristics (see Section 4.6.2). In phase two, we try to identify a feasible solution to the MCLPP in the vicinity of each estimated dominating loading-plan set.

We generate two classes of test data, corresponding to two different application scenarios from Section 4.6, based on historical data provided by the audio equipment manufacturer. We conduct extensive computational experiments to demonstrate the effectiveness of our approach.

To our best knowledge, there is no literature concerned with the MCLPP. However, the MCLPP can be considered an extension of the Multiple Container Loading Cost Minimization Problem (MCLCMP). The major difference between the MCLPP and the MCLCMP is that, in the MCLPP, the purchase order can be changed slightly according to product preference. Another significant feature of the MCLPP is that products are associated with preferences. Product preference is closely related to the concept of loading priority described by Bischoff and Ratcliff [4]. Ren et al. [77] studied the single container loading problem with an absolute loading priority constraint. However, as far as we know, no paper explicitly discusses the multiple-container loading problem with a loading priority constraint.

4.2 Problem Definition

In the MCLPP, the initial order is represented by a vector $\boldsymbol{b}$, where $b_i > 0$ is the quantity of product $i, i = 1, \cdots, N$. The preferences of these products are stored in a vector $\boldsymbol{p}$, where $p_i > 0$ is the preference of product $i, i = 1, \cdots, N$. A vector $\boldsymbol{c}$ is used to denote the costs of available containers, where $c_t > 0$ is the cost of a type t container ($t = 1, \cdots, T$). As described in Section 4.1, we need to change the order quantity (resulting in an adjusted order) and load all items of the adjusted order into a set of containers, such that the shipping cost per unit preference is minimized. The shipping cost per unit preference is defined as the total shipping cost over the total preference of loaded items, where the total shipping cost only includes the cost of the containers used.

We denote the adjusted order with $\boldsymbol{y}$, where y_i is the quantity of product i. A change to the order quantity is acceptable only if the following **adjustment requirements** are met:

- **Unidirectional Adjustment:** Either $\boldsymbol{y} \geqslant \boldsymbol{b}$ or $\boldsymbol{y} \leqslant \boldsymbol{b}$.
- **No Piggyback:** Products not in the initial order cannot be introduced into the adjusted order. This constraint will make a difference in certain situations. For example, if a manufacturer produces a relatively stable category of products, it is possible to accelerate the generation of shipping plans by conducting a preprocessing algorithm. The preprocessing must take this requirement into consideration.
- **Bounded Quantity:** There is a lower bound and an upper bound on $y_i, \forall i = 1, \cdots, N$. If all lower bounds are represented by vector $\underline{\boldsymbol{b}}$ and all upper bounds are represented by $\overline{\boldsymbol{b}}$, we must have $\underline{\boldsymbol{b}} \leqslant \boldsymbol{y} \leqslant \overline{\boldsymbol{b}}$.

Assume that all items are packaged in 3D rectangular boxes; thus, the terms *item* and *box* will be used interchangeably through the rest of this chapter. The dimensions of a type i box are given by l_i, w_i and h_i, while the dimensions of the loading space in a type t container are given by L_t, W_t and H_t. Therefore, the *per-item volume* of type i boxes is defined as $v_i = l_i w_i h_i$ and the volume of a type t container is defined as $V_t = L_t W_t H_t$. We use a vector $v \in \mathbb{R}_+^N$ to store all per-item volumes. Given an order and a set of containers, we define a **loading plan** as a valid geometric layout for loading the items from the order into the containers. A geometric layout is valid if and only if the following **loading constraints** are satisfied:

- **No empty container:** Each container must contain at least one box.
- **Containment:** Each box must be fully contained by one and only one container.
- **Orthogonal Placement:** Each box must be placed with its edges parallel to those of the container it is in.
- **No Overlap:** Any two boxes inside the same container do not overlap with each other.
- **Orientation Restriction:** Every box must be placed in one of its allowed orientations. In reality, not all products can be freely rotated. For example, certain types of audio equipment must be placed vertically because of fragile sides. In our problem, we use three flags (f_i^l , f_i^w , and f_i^h , respectively) to indicate whether product i can be placed with its length, width, and height aligned with the vertical axis of a container. If $f_i^h = 1$, product i can be placed with its height aligned with the vertical axis. If all three flags are set at 1, the product can be freely rotated.

In addition, we ignore the availability of containers, which means we assume that the quantity of each type of container is infinite. This is because purchase orders normally have small sizes compared to the container capacity of typical logistics service providers.

4.3 The MCLPP is a Generalized Container Loading Problem

In the generalized container loading problem, we are given a set of three-dimensional containers denoted by $\mathcal{J}$. Each container $j \in \mathcal{J}$ has the cost C_j . Containers with the same dimensions and cost belong to the same type, and the types of containers are stored in the set $\mathcal{T}$. LB_t and UB_t denote the minimum and maximum number of containers of type $t \in \mathcal{T}$ that can be selected, and UB

denotes the maximum number of containers of all types that can be used.

We are also given K sets of three-dimensional items. $\mathcal{J}_k$ is used to denote the k-th set of items, $\forall k = 1,\ldots,K$. Each item $i \in \mathcal{J}_k$ has the value v_i. Any set of items $\mathcal{J}_k$ can be divided into two subsets in this problem: the subset of mandatory items, denoted by $\mathcal{J}_k^M$, and the subset of optional items, denoted by $\mathcal{J}_k^O$, which is equal to $\mathcal{J}_k^M \setminus \mathcal{J}_k^M$.

We need to select one set of items and load all of its mandatory items, together with some or all of its optional items, into the limited number of container (s), such that the unit shipping cost is minimized. The unit shipping cost is defined as the quotient of the total cost of the selected containers and the total value of the loaded items.

The MCLPP can be proved to be a generalized container loading problem by considering that:

- There is no limitation on container availability: $UB_t = \infty$, $LB_t = 0$, and $UB = \infty$.
- There are two sets of items: $\mathcal{J}_1$ and $\mathcal{J}_2$. Item set $\mathcal{J}_1$ consists of N types of products, and the number of Product i in $\mathcal{J}_1$ is $b_i, \forall i = 1,\cdots,N$. Similarly, item set $\mathcal{J}_2$ consists of the same N types of products as $\mathcal{J}_1$, but the number of Product i in $\mathcal{J}_2$ is $\bar{b}_i, \forall i = 1,\cdots,N$.
- In item set $\mathcal{J}_1$, the group of mandatory items $\mathcal{J}_1^M$ is composed of N types of products, and the number of Product i in $\mathcal{J}_1^M$ is $\underline{b}_i, \forall\ i = 1,\cdots,N$. The remaining products in set $\mathcal{J}_1$ form the optional item group $\mathcal{J}_1^O$.
- In item set $\mathcal{J}_2$, the group of mandatory items $\mathcal{J}_2^M$ is composed of N types of products, and the number of Product i in $\mathcal{J}_2^M$ is $b_i, \forall i = 1,\cdots,N$. The remaining products in set $\mathcal{J}_2$ form the optional item group $\mathcal{J}_2^O$.
- The value of a product i in either set $\mathcal{J}_1$ or set $\mathcal{J}_2$ is its preference p_i.

Since the value of a product is represented by its preference, the objective function of this generalized problem becomes minimizing the quotient of the total cost of used containers and the total preference of loaded products, which is exactly the same objective as that of the MCLPP.

Item sets $\mathcal{J}_1$ and $\mathcal{J}_2$ are not independent because $\mathcal{J}_1 \subset \mathcal{J}_2$ and $\mathcal{J}_1 = \mathcal{J}_2^M$. It is better to merge the two sets $\mathcal{J}_1$ and $\mathcal{J}_2$ to solve the problem. Therefore, we introduce a new combinatorial formulation to model the MCLPP, rather than employing the general model and the set-covering model of the generalized container loading problem.

4.4 A Combinatorial Formulation

Let $\boldsymbol{y}$ be an N-dimensional column vector, whose element y_i is the quantity of the i-th product in the purchase order, and let $\boldsymbol{x}$ be a T-dimensional column vector, where x_t is the number of type t containers, $t = 1,\cdots,T$. If all products denoted by $\boldsymbol{y}$ can be loaded into the set of containers denoted by $\boldsymbol{x}$, while respecting all the loading constraints in Section 4.2, we call the pair $(\boldsymbol{x},\boldsymbol{y})$ a **loading plan** and denote it with $\mathcal{L}(\boldsymbol{x},\boldsymbol{y})$. The shipping cost associated with $\mathcal{L}(\boldsymbol{x},\boldsymbol{y})$ is given by $\boldsymbol{c}^T\boldsymbol{x}$, and the total preference of products is given by $\boldsymbol{p}^T\boldsymbol{y}$. Furthermore, we define a loading plan $\mathcal{L}(\boldsymbol{x},\boldsymbol{y})$ to be feasible for the MCLPP if $\boldsymbol{y}$ satisfies all adjustment requirements in Section 4.2. Then, the set of all feasible loading plans is given by:

$$\mathcal{F}=\left\{\mathcal{L}\left(\boldsymbol{x},\boldsymbol{y}\right)|\boldsymbol{b}\leqslant\boldsymbol{y}\leqslant\bar{\boldsymbol{b}}\vee\underline{\boldsymbol{b}}\leqslant\boldsymbol{y}\leqslant\boldsymbol{b},\boldsymbol{x}\in\mathbb{Z}_+^T,\boldsymbol{y}\in\mathbb{Z}_+^N\right\}$$

We group loading plans with the same shipping costs and total preferences into a **loading-plan** set as follows:

$$\mathcal{S}(C,P)=\left\{\mathcal{L}\left(\boldsymbol{x},\boldsymbol{y}\right)|\boldsymbol{c}^T\boldsymbol{x}=C,\boldsymbol{p}^T\boldsymbol{y}=P,\boldsymbol{x}\in\mathbb{Z}_+^T,\boldsymbol{y}\in\mathbb{Z}_+^N\right\}$$

We say a loading-plan set is feasible if it contains at least one feasible loading plan (i.e., $\mathcal{S}(C,P)\cap\mathcal{F}\neq\phi$). Therefore, given a feasible loading-plan set $\mathcal{S}(C,P)$, we must have $C\in\mathcal{C}$ and $P\in\mathcal{P}$ where:

$$\mathcal{C}=\left\{C|C=\boldsymbol{c}^T\boldsymbol{\alpha},\boldsymbol{\alpha}\in\mathbb{Z}_+^T\right\}$$

$$\mathcal{P}=\left\{P|\boldsymbol{p}^T\underline{\boldsymbol{b}}\leqslant P\leqslant\boldsymbol{p}^T\bar{\boldsymbol{b}},P=\boldsymbol{p}^T\boldsymbol{\beta},\boldsymbol{\beta}\in\mathbb{Z}_+^N\right\}$$

Obviously, every feasible solution to the MCLPP corresponds to some feasible loading plan $\mathcal{L}(x,y)$ that lies in some feasible loading-plan set $\mathcal{S}(C,P)$. Therefore, the objective value of an optimal solution to the MCLPP can be found by solving the following constrained maximization problem:

MCLPP: Minimize $\dfrac{C}{P}$

subject to

$$\mathcal{S}(C,P) \cap \mathcal{F} \neq \phi$$

We proceed to analyze the feasible region of model **MCLPP**. Suppose a nonempty loading-plan set $\mathcal{S}(C,P)$ can be represented by a circle centered at point (C,P) of a preference-cost plane. Then, all feasible loading-plan sets lie in the shaded area of Figure 4.1.

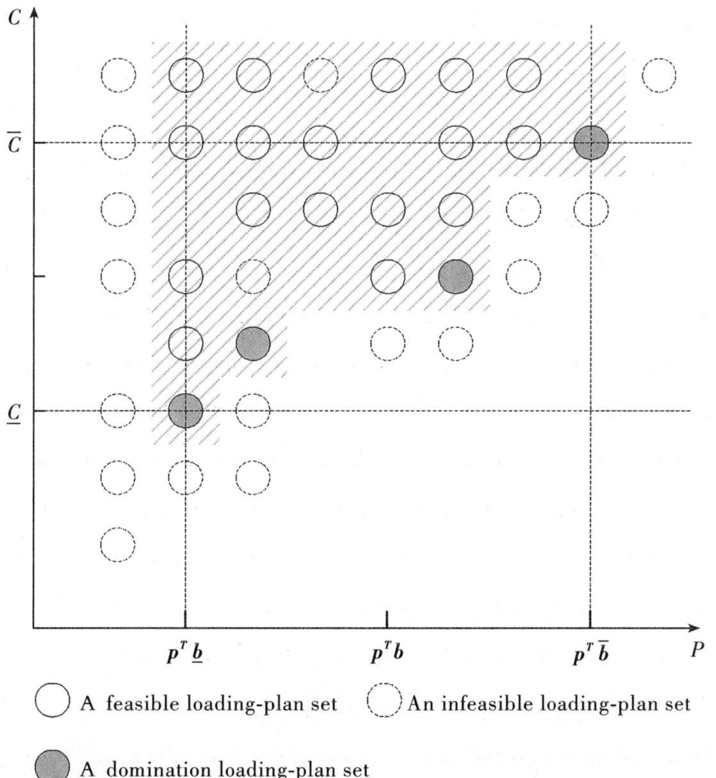

Figure 4.1 Feasible region of model MCLPP on the Preference-Cost plane. Every circle centered at (C,P) represents a non-empty loading-plan set $\mathcal{S}(C,P)$

Given a feasible loading-plan set $\mathcal{S}(C,P)$, we must have $P \in \mathcal{P}$. Thus, the left and right boundaries of the shaded area are given by the vertical lines $P = \boldsymbol{p}^T \underline{\boldsymbol{b}}$ and $P = \boldsymbol{p}^T \overline{\boldsymbol{b}}$, respectively.

The bottom boundary of the shaded area is a staircase determined by the dominating loading-plan sets (gray circles), which are defined as follows:

Definition 4.1 A feasible loading-plan set $\mathcal{S}(C,P)$ dominates another feasible loading-plan set $\mathcal{S}(C',P')$ if $C \leqslant C' \wedge P \geqslant P'$ and at least one inequality is strict. A feasible loading-plan set that is not dominated by any other feasible loading-plan set is called a **dominating loading-plan set**.

Let $\underline{C}$ and $\overline{C}$ be the minimum total costs of containers that can accommodate all products denoted by $\boldsymbol{y} = \underline{\boldsymbol{b}}$ and $\boldsymbol{y} = \overline{\boldsymbol{b}}$, respectively. It is clear from Figure 4.1 that no feasible loading-plan set lies below the horizontal line $C = \underline{C}$ and that all feasible loading-plan sets above the horizontal line $C = \overline{C}$ are dominated. Therefore, all dominating sets lie between line $C = \underline{C}$ and line $C = \overline{C}$.

Given the definition of a domination loading-plan set, it is obvious that every optimal solution to the MCLPP must lie in one of the dominating loading-plan sets. As a result, it is sufficient to explore only the dominating loading-plan sets to identify an optimal solution to the MCLPP. This observation forms the basis of our heuristic algorithm, which is described in the next section.

All circles in Figure 4.1 between the vertical lines $\boldsymbol{p}^T \underline{\boldsymbol{b}}$ and $\boldsymbol{p}^T \boldsymbol{b}$ include solutions in which only items from set $\mathcal{J}_1$ are loaded into containers, while circles between the vertical lines $\boldsymbol{p}^T \boldsymbol{b}$ and $\boldsymbol{p}^T \overline{\boldsymbol{b}}$ include solutions in which only items from set $\mathcal{J}_2$ are loaded into containers. Correspondingly, circles on line $\boldsymbol{p}^T \underline{\boldsymbol{b}}$ include solutions in which only mandatory items of set $\mathcal{J}_1$ are loaded, while circles on line $\boldsymbol{p}^T \boldsymbol{b}$ include solutions in which only mandatory items of set $\mathcal{J}_2$ are loaded.

4.5 A Two-Phase Heuristic

The main challenge in solving the MCLPP is determining whether a loading - plan set $\mathcal{S}(C,P)$ contains feasible solutions. If we can quickly determine whether a loading - plan set is feasible, we can enumerate the dominating loading-plan sets quickly and rank them in decreasing order of C/P. Searching for an optimal solution to the MCLPP is then reduced to searching for a feasible solution in the dominating loading-plan set with the largest C/P.

Determining whether a loading-plan set contains a feasible solution is a very difficult decision problem. It contains the sub-problem of determining feasible 3D geometric layouts of products inside containers. We, therefore, propose a two-phase heuristic for the MCLPP. In the first phase, we try to estimate the lower boundary of the shaded area in Figure 4.1. That is to say, we employ a heuristic strategy to identify loading-plan sets that are likely to be dominating. In the second phase, we search for a best feasible solution in the vicinity of those loading-plan sets by solving a series of 3D orthogonal packing sub-problems.

4.5.1 Phase One: Estimate Dominating Loading-plan Sets

From Figure 4.1, we can see that a dominating loading-plan set must be the right-most circle in the row $C \in \mathcal{C} \cap [\underline{C}, \overline{C}]$. Therefore, we estimate dominating loading-plan sets in the following two steps.

(1) Enumerate All Rows Containing Dominating Loading-Plan Sets

Searching for $\underline{C}$ could be a highly complicated problem. Instead, we find its lower bound by solving the following minimization problem:

EC_lb: Minimize $C = \boldsymbol{c}^T \boldsymbol{x}$ (4.1)

subject to

$$\boldsymbol{u}^T \boldsymbol{x} \geqslant \boldsymbol{v}^T \underline{\boldsymbol{b}} \tag{4.2}$$

$$\boldsymbol{x} \in \mathbb{Z}_+^T \tag{4.3}$$

Constraint 4.2 requires that the total usable volume of selected containers is larger than the total volume of products denoted by $\underline{\boldsymbol{b}}$. It is obvious that Constraint 4.2 ignores the geometric layout of packing; thus, the optimal objective value, denoted as $\underline{C}^e$, is a lower bound of $\underline{C}$.

Similarly, we calculate an upper bound for $\overline{C}$ by solving the following minimization problem:

EC_ub: Minimize $C = \sum_{t=1}^{T} c_t x_t$ (4.4)

subject to

$$\sum_{t=1}^{T} m_{ti} z_{ti} \geqslant \overline{b}_i, \forall i = 1, \cdots, N \tag{4.5}$$

$$\sum_{i=1}^{N} z_{ti} = x_t, \forall t = 1, \cdots, T \tag{4.6}$$

$$x_t \in \mathbb{Z}_+, \forall T = 1, \cdots, T \tag{4.7}$$

$$z_{ti} \in \mathbb{Z}_+, \forall t = 1, \cdots, T, i = 1, \cdots, N \tag{4.8}$$

$m_{ti} = \lfloor L_t / l_i \rfloor \times \lfloor W_t / w_i \rfloor \times \lfloor H_t / h_i \rfloor$. It is clear that m_{ti} is the minimum number of type i products that can be loaded into a type t container with a fixed orientation. Therefore, Constraint 4.5 guarantees that all products represented by $\overline{\boldsymbol{b}}$ can be loaded into the selected containers. We denote the optimal objective value as $\overline{C}^e$.

Since $[\underline{C}, \overline{C}]$ is included in $[\underline{C}^e, \overline{C}^e]$, we can enumerate $\mathcal{C} \cap [\underline{C}, \overline{C}]$ by enumerating all rows in $\mathcal{C} \cap [\underline{C}^e, \overline{C}^e]$ This can be done efficiently by adapting an algorithm for the integral knapsack problem (see Algorithm 4.1).

(2) Estimate the Right-most Circle in a Row

For each row $C \in \mathcal{C} \cap [\underline{C}^e, \overline{C}^e]$, we need to search for the set of products with maximum total preference that can be loaded into containers with a total cost C. Searching for the most preferred set of products is a difficult sub-

Algorithm 4.1 Enumerate All Rows C in $\mathcal{C}\cap[\underline{C}^e,\overline{C}^e]$

EnumRow $(\boldsymbol{c},\underline{C}^e,\overline{C}^e)$

// ***Input***: $\boldsymbol{c}$: container costs

// $\underline{C}^e,\overline{C}^e$: enumeration boundaries

$R=\phi$

$Q=\phi$

Add all distinct c_t into Q

While $Q\neq\phi$

  cur=remove the smallest from Q

  if $cur\geqslant\underline{C}^e$

    add *cur* to R

  for each c_t

    $next=cur+c_t$

    if $next\leqslant\overline{C}^e$ and $next\notin Q$

      add *next* to Q

return R

problem because, in a typical MCLPP instance, there may be several combinations of containers with the same total shipping cost C. Moreover, we need to load products with maximum total preference into each container combination, which is a generalization of the well-studied Single Container Loading Problem (SCLP). It is well known that SCLP is a very difficult optimization problem. The state-of-the-art SCLP algorithm takes a few seconds to hundreds of seconds on a modern computer to find a high-quality solution [90].

We, therefore, opt to estimate the rightmost circle of a row using a heuristic strategy. When loading products into a container, we ignore the three-dimensional shape of the products. Ignoring the three-dimensional shape usually leads to an over-estimation of the volume utilization of a container. Take the well-known benchmark test instance for SCLP (i.e., BR15) as an example. The state-of-the-art SCLP algorithm ID-GLTS by

[90] is only capable of finding solutions with an average volume utilization below 94%. If we ignore the three-dimensional shape of small items, the average volume utilization of containers is well beyond 99%. To accurately estimate the dominating loading-plan sets, we need to take the over-estimation of container volume utilization into account. Specifically, we should determine the true volume utilization of each container.

It is well known that the volume utilization of each container in a packing problem is closely related to the heterogeneity of the box assortment. For example, Table 4.1 summarizes the performance of leading SCLP algorithms.

Table 4.1 Performance of leading SCLP algorithms on 15 BR test sets, as reported in [90]. Each cell represents the percentage of utilized volume in a container, averaged over 100 instances in a test set

Test set	GRASP (2005)	IC (2005)	FDA (2011)	VNS (2010)	CLTRS (2010)	G2LA (2010)	ID-GLTS (2012)
BR1	89.07	91.60	92.92	94.93	95.05	95.54	95.55
BR2	90.43	91.99	93.93	95.19	95.43	95.98	96.08
BR3	90.86	92.30	93.71	94.99	95.47	96.08	96.24
BR4	90.42	92.36	93.68	94.71	95.18	95.94	96.07
BR5	89.57	91.90	93.73	94.33	95.00	95.74	95.94
BR6	89.71	91.51	93.63	94.04	94.79	95.61	95.72
BR7	88.05	91.01	93.14	93.53	94.24	95.14	95.28
BR8	86.13	—	92.92	92.78	93.70	94.63	94.71
BR9	85.08	—	92.49	92.19	93.44	94.29	94.46
BR10	84.21	—	92.24	91.92	93.09	94.05	94.27
BR11	83.98	—	91.91	91.46	92.81	93.78	94.09
BR12	83.64	—	91.83	91.20	92.73	93.67	94.03
BR13	83.54	—	91.56	91.11	92.46	93.54	93.80
BR14	83.25	—	91.30	90.64	92.40	93.36	93.76
BR15	83.21	—	91.02	90.38	92.40	93.32	93.72

As we can see, the average volume utilization of solutions produced by each algorithm decreases as the number of product types increases from 3 in test set BR1 to 100 in BR15.

This trend generally holds in other packing problems. The size of products relative to the size of a container also affects the container's volume utilization. When products are small compared to a container, we can expect that the container is densely packed (if there are sufficient products), since holes can be easily filled. This implies that we can achieve denser packing in 40-foot containers than in 20-foot ones. Therefore, the volume utilization of each container should be estimated based on both the heterogeneity of the box assortment and the container type.

In an MCLPP application, it is reasonable to expect that the manufacturer produces a relatively stable category of products and that its customers order a relative stable set of products. Furthermore, the types of containers used by the manufacturer are usually fixed. Therefore, it is sensible to estimate the volume utilization of containers using statistics from historical data. Given the estimated volume utilization, we can calculate the usable volume of each container.

Let $\boldsymbol{u}$ be a column vector, where u_t is the estimated usable volume of a type t container. Let $\boldsymbol{x}$ denote a set of containers and let $\boldsymbol{y}$ denote a set of products in a customer's order. Assuming we are only allowed to vary $\boldsymbol{y}$ within the bounds $\underline{\boldsymbol{d}}$ and $\overline{\boldsymbol{d}}$, the maximal preference of products we can ship within a total cost C can be estimated by solving the following maximization problem:

EP$\left(C,\underline{\boldsymbol{d}},\overline{\boldsymbol{d}}\right)$: Maximize $P=\boldsymbol{p}^T\boldsymbol{y}$ (4.9)

subject to

$$\boldsymbol{c}^T\boldsymbol{x}=C \tag{4.10}$$

$$\boldsymbol{u}^T\boldsymbol{x}\geqslant\boldsymbol{v}^T\boldsymbol{y} \tag{4.11}$$

$$\underline{\boldsymbol{d}}\leqslant\boldsymbol{y}\leqslant\overline{\boldsymbol{d}} \tag{4.12}$$

$$\boldsymbol{x}\in\mathbb{Z}_+^T \tag{4.13}$$

$$\boldsymbol{y}\in\mathbb{Z}_+^N \tag{4.14}$$

Constraint 4.10 requires that the costs of selected containers sum up to C. Constraint 4.11 requires that the total usable volume of selected containers be larger than the total volume of products so that the set of products has a good chance of being able to be loaded into the selected container. Let $\boldsymbol{x}^*$, $\boldsymbol{y}^*$ be an optimal solution to **EP** ($C,\underline{\boldsymbol{d}},\bar{\boldsymbol{d}}$). It is possible that we cannot load all products denoted by y^* into containers denoted by $\boldsymbol{x}^*$; therefore, the solution to **EP** ($C,\underline{\boldsymbol{d}},\bar{\boldsymbol{d}}$)can serve only as an estimation.

Since we are allowed to adjust the initial customer order either upwards or downwards, the P corresponding to the rightmost circle in a row C can be estimated by solving the maximization problem **EP**, at most, twice. First, we try to solve **EP** ($C,\boldsymbol{b},\bar{\boldsymbol{b}}$). If there is no feasible solution, we next try to solve **EP** ($C,\underline{\boldsymbol{b}},\boldsymbol{b}$).

Accordingly, our phase-one heuristic is summarized in Algorithm 4.2.

Algorithm 4.2 **Estimate Dominating Loading-plan Sets**

EstDomPatSets ( )

// **Data:** $\boldsymbol{c}$: container costs

// $\boldsymbol{b}$: initial customer order

// $\underline{\boldsymbol{b}},\bar{\boldsymbol{b}}$: lower and upper bounds for valid order

// $\boldsymbol{p}$: product preferences

$\underline{C}$ = solve **EC_lb** using CPLEX

$\bar{C}$ = solve **EC_ub** using CPLEX

$\mathcal{C}$ EnumRows ($\boldsymbol{c},\underline{C},\bar{C}$)

$R = \phi$ //enumerated rows

for each $C \in \mathcal{C}$

  $(\boldsymbol{x}^*,\boldsymbol{y}^*)$ = solve **EP** ($C,\boldsymbol{b},\bar{\boldsymbol{b}}$) using CPLEX

  if no feasible solution is found

    $(\boldsymbol{x}^*,\boldsymbol{y}^*)$ = solve **EP** ($C,\underline{\boldsymbol{b}},\boldsymbol{b}$) using CPLEX

  if a solution is found

    Add $(\boldsymbol{x}^*,\boldsymbol{y}^*)$ to R

Sort all pairs $(\boldsymbol{x}^*,\boldsymbol{y}^*)$ in R in ascending order of $\frac{\boldsymbol{c}^T\boldsymbol{x}^*}{\boldsymbol{p}^T\boldsymbol{y}^*}$

return R

Remark: It is obvious from Figure 4.1 that a dominating loading-plan set also corresponds to the bottommost circle in a column. Therefore, an alternative approach is to enumerate dominating loading-plan sets column-wise. That is, we try to estimate the minimal cost of containers that can accommodate products with the total preference $P \in \mathcal{P}$. It is reasonable to assume its difficulty is similar to that of **EP**. The main reason that we prefer row-wise enumeration over column-wise enumeration is that there are many fewer rows than columns in an MCLPP instance. Typically, there are only three container types, but dozens of product types, which means that the possible product combinations easily outnumber the possible container combinations.

4.5.2 Phase Two: Search Within Dominating Loading-plan Sets

By the end of phase one, we have identified a list of pairs $(\boldsymbol{x}^*, \boldsymbol{y}^*)$, each representing a loading-plan set $\mathcal{S}(C,P)$ with $C = \boldsymbol{c}^T \boldsymbol{x}^*$ and $P = \boldsymbol{p}^T \boldsymbol{y}^*$. Each loading-plan set is likely to contain a feasible solution to the MCLPP. The loading-plan sets are sorted in ascending order of C/P. In phase two, we consider the first K loading-plan sets $\mathcal{S}(C,P)$ in the ordered list. For each loading-plan set $\mathcal{S}(C,P)$, we try to identify a feasible solution using a heuristic strategy.

There may be several container combinations with the same total cost C, and there may be many product combinations with the same total preference P. Among all container combinations, the one with the largest usable volume dominates the others, in the sense that this combination is most likely to accommodate more products and, hence, increase total preference. Similarly, among all product combinations, the one with the least total volume dominates the others, in the sense that this combination is most likely to be accommodated by a given set of containers. Therefore, in the process of searching for a feasible solution, we tend to pick the set of containers with the largest total usable volume and the set of products with the smallest total volume.

It is reasonable to use $(\boldsymbol{x}^*, \boldsymbol{y}^*)$ as our initial guess and to search for a best-order $\boldsymbol{y}$ that can be accommodated in the containers $\boldsymbol{x}^*$. We apply a binary search to the total box volume to determine an order $\boldsymbol{y}$ (see Algorithm4.3).

Algorithm 4.3 Find Best-Order $\boldsymbol{y}$ for Containers $\boldsymbol{x}^*$ Using Binary Search on Total Volume

---

Binary Search $(\boldsymbol{x}^*, M, \underline{\boldsymbol{d}}, \overline{\boldsymbol{d}})$

// Data: $\boldsymbol{c}$: container costs

// $\boldsymbol{v}$: product box volumes

// $\boldsymbol{V}$: container volumes

// $\boldsymbol{b}$: initial customer order

// $\underline{\boldsymbol{b}}, \overline{\boldsymbol{b}}$: lower and upper bounds for valid order

// $\boldsymbol{p}$: product preferences

// Input: $\boldsymbol{x}^*$: $C = \boldsymbol{c}^T \boldsymbol{x}^*$ is the row we want to search

// $\underline{\boldsymbol{d}}, \overline{\boldsymbol{d}}$: search range

$\boldsymbol{y} = 0$ // the best known order

$L = \boldsymbol{v}^T \underline{\boldsymbol{d}}$

$U = \min\{\boldsymbol{V}^T \boldsymbol{x}^*, \boldsymbol{v}^T \overline{\boldsymbol{d}}\}$

$\epsilon = \min\{v_i \mid i = 1, 2, \cdots, N\}$

while $U - L > \epsilon$

  // Identify the most preferred order $\boldsymbol{s}$ with total volume $\leqslant M$

  $\boldsymbol{s} =$ optimal solution to SO$(M, \underline{\boldsymbol{d}}, \overline{\boldsymbol{d}})$

  // Load as many products as possible into containers $\boldsymbol{x}^*$

  $\boldsymbol{s}' =$ GreedyLoad $(\boldsymbol{x}^*, \boldsymbol{s})$

  if $\underline{\boldsymbol{b}} \leqslant \boldsymbol{s}' \leqslant \boldsymbol{b}$ or $\boldsymbol{b} \leqslant \boldsymbol{s}' \leqslant \overline{\boldsymbol{b}}$

    if $\boldsymbol{p}^T \boldsymbol{s}' > \boldsymbol{p}^T \boldsymbol{y}$

      $\boldsymbol{y} = \boldsymbol{s}'$

  if $\boldsymbol{s}' = \boldsymbol{s}$ // All products are loaded

    $L = M$

  else $U = M$

  $M = (U + L)/2$

续表

```
return y
GreedyLoad (x*, y)
    s = 0 // loaded products
    cList ← sort containers x* in descending order of volumes
    for each container C in cList
        // Load as many boxes as possible into the container C
        b = SCLP (C, y)
        s = s + b
        y = y − b
    return s
```

The problem **SO** is defined as follows:

$$\mathrm{SO}(V, \underline{\boldsymbol{d}}, \overline{\boldsymbol{d}}):\quad \text{Maximize}\quad \boldsymbol{p}^T\boldsymbol{y} \tag{4.15}$$

subject to

$$\boldsymbol{v}^T\boldsymbol{y} \leqslant V \tag{4.16}$$

$$\underline{\boldsymbol{d}} \leqslant \boldsymbol{y} \leqslant \overline{\boldsymbol{d}} \tag{4.17}$$

$$\boldsymbol{y} \in \mathbb{Z}_+^N \tag{4.18}$$

where $\underline{\boldsymbol{d}}$, $\overline{\boldsymbol{d}}$ define the allowed range for an order. The optimal solution to **SO** is an order $\boldsymbol{y}$ with a total box volume not exceeding V that maximizes total preference.

To check whether an order $\boldsymbol{y}$ can be loaded into a set of containers $\boldsymbol{x}$, we invoke sub-routine GreedyLoad. It loads the containers one at a time in a greedy manner and returns a vector representing the set of products loaded. The single container loading algorithm SCLP used in GreedyLoad is adapted from the Iterative-Doubling Greedy 1-step Lookahead Algorithm (ID-G1LA) proposed by Zhu et al. [90]. The only difference between our SCLP and ID-G1LA is that we evaluate a (partial) solution using the total preference of boxes loaded instead of total volume. We briefly introduce the ID-G1LA. For complete details, we refer the readers to [90].

The ID-G1LA is a block building approach; that is, the boxes are first arranged into compact blocks, and then packing solutions are constructed by loading blocks instead of individual boxes. Beginning with an empty container and a list of candidate blocks, a block is selected and placed at one of the corners of the container in each step. The remaining free space in the container is represented as a list of cuboids called **residual spaces**. In the subsequent steps, a residual space and one of the available blocks are selected, and the selected block is placed at a corner of the selected space. After this, the lists of residual spaces and candidate blocks are updated. This process is repeated until the list of residual spaces is empty, whereupon a feasible loading plan is found. A tree search procedure is used to generate several feasible loading plans, and the one maximizing objective function is returned.

Our phase two heuristic is summarized in Algorithm 4.4 Given a loading-plan set $\mathcal{S}(C,P)$ with $C=\boldsymbol{c}^T\boldsymbol{x}^*$ and $P=\boldsymbol{p}^T\boldsymbol{y}^*$, we will invoke binary search, at most, twice to search for a feasible solution $\boldsymbol{x}^*$, $\boldsymbol{y}^*$. When the estimated order $\boldsymbol{y}^*$ in phase one is larger than the initial order $\boldsymbol{b}$, we search for an order in the range between $\boldsymbol{b}$ and $\bar{\boldsymbol{b}}$, starting at $\boldsymbol{y}^*$ (line 6). If we fail to find a feasible solution, we try to search for an order in the range between $\underline{\boldsymbol{b}}$ and $\boldsymbol{b}$, starting at the middle point (line 10). When the estimated order $\boldsymbol{y}^*$ is smaller than the initial order $\boldsymbol{b}$, we only search in the range between $\underline{\boldsymbol{b}}$ and $\boldsymbol{b}$, starting at the middle point (line 11).

Algorithm 4.4 Find Feasible Solution in the Vicinity of Dominating Sets

SearchAroundDomPlanSets (R)

// **Data:** $\boldsymbol{v}$: product box volumes

// $\boldsymbol{b}$: initial customer order

// $\underline{\boldsymbol{b}}$,$\bar{\boldsymbol{b}}$: lower and upper bounds for valid order

//Input: R: list of pairs $(\boldsymbol{x},\boldsymbol{y})$ representing loading-plan sets $\mathcal{S}(\boldsymbol{c}^T\boldsymbol{x},\boldsymbol{p}^T\boldsymbol{y})$

续表

$x^* = 0, y^* = 0, f = \infty$
for the i-th pair $(x, y) \in R$
  if $i < K$
    $s = 0$
    if $y \geqslant b$
      $s =$ BinarySearch $(x, v^T y, v^T b, v^T \bar{b})$
      if $s == 0$
        $L = v^T \underline{b}$
        $U = v^T b$
          $s =$ BinarySearch $(x, (L + U)/2, L, U)$
    else $s =$ BinarySearch $(x, v^T y, v^T b, v^T \bar{b})$
  // Try to update best know solution
    if $s > 0$ and $\frac{c^T x}{v^T s} < f$
      $x^* = x$
      $y^* = s$
      $f = \frac{c^T x}{v^T s}$
      $i = i + 1$
return(x^*, y^*, f)

4.6 Computational Experiments

Our two-phase heuristic approach was implemented as a sequential algorithm in Java (JDK 7 updated 21, 64-bit edition), and no multi-threading was explicitly used. All experiments described in this section were conducted on a personal computer equipped with an Intel Core (TM) i7-3770 CPU clocked at 3.40 gigahertz and an 8 gigabyte RAM, running a Windows 7 (64-bit) operating system. The commercial integer linear programming solver used was the IBM ILog CPLEX Optimization Studio 12.2 (64-bit) with its default settings.

Since there is no standard benchmark, we generated 20 sets of MCLPP instances based on historical data provided by a manufacturer to test the effectiveness of our approach. The details are presented in Section 4.6.1.

We calibrated our two-phase approach by selecting an appropriate estimation for the usable volume of each container and deciding on suitable values for the parameters involved, which are presented in Section 4.6.2 to 4.6.3 and Section 4.6.4, respectively. Finally, we demonstrate the performance of our approach on all MCLPP instances in Section 4.6.5.

4.6.1 Generate Test Instances

We collected 12-month purchase order data from a company in Hong Kong. A total of 2 187 products are shipped by the company, and each product is packaged into a carton box. Most orders consist of N products, with N coming from the set {3, 5, 8, 13, 15, 16, 17, 19, 25, 26}. No product preference is utilized in the company's current practice. Discussion with the logistic officer suggests that the following two settings are reasonable:

- **Quantity-Based Preference (QBP):** The preference of each product is proportional to its quantity, $p_i = b_i / \sum_{i=1}^{N} b_i$.

- **Volume-Based Preference (VBP):** The preference of each product is proportional to its volume, $p_i = v_i / \sum_{i=1}^{N} v_i$.

Currently, three types of containers are frequently used by the company: namely, 20-foot standard, 40-foot standard, and 40-foot high cube containers. Their dimensions are given in Table 4.2. The price for each container is extracted from 11.

Table 4.2 Container information

Type	Length (cm)	Width (cm)	Height (cm)	Unit Price ($)
20'standard	590	235	239	900
40'standard	1 203	235	239	1 700
40'highcube	1 203	235	270	1 800

We generated two classes of MCLPP instances, one for each preference setting, and we call them class QBP and class VBP, respectively. The two classes of instances differ only in how we set preferences for products. Each class consists of 10 instance sets, one for each $N \in \{3,5,8,13,15,16,17,19,25,26\}$. The 10 sets in class QBP are named QBP03, QBP05, ..., QBP26; the 10 sets in class VBP are named VBP03, VBP05, ..., VBP26. Each set consists of 50 randomly generated instances.

An instance is generated as follows. We first set a target V for the total volume of products in an order. The target volume is uniformly randomly generated so that the order will require between 5 to 20 20-foot standard containers. We then uniformly randomly select N products out of the 2 187 products and initialize their quantities to 1. Next, we uniformly randomly select one product out of the N products and increase its quantity by 1. We repeatedly increase the order quantity until the total volume of all products in the order exceeds the target volume V. For all the generated instances, we assume that all three types of containers can be utilized and that all products can be freely rotated.

4.6.2 Estimate Usable Volume via Statistics

A unique feature of our approach is that we try to estimate the average capability of the SCLP sub-routine and take it into account in overall planning. To obtain a useful estimate, we randomly generate a large set of SCLP instances that are statistically similar to the historical order data. Our domain knowledge in packing suggests that box heterogeneity and container dimensions are the two of the most important characteristics affecting volume utilization.

We generate three classes of SCLP instances—20S, 40S, and 40H—one for each container type. For each class, we generate 10 sets of instances, one for each $N \in \{3,5,8,13,15,16,17,19,25,26\}$. Instances in the same test set consist of the same number of products per order. We name a test set by appending a hyphen ('–') and two digits corresponding to N to the class name. For example, all instances in the test set 20S –26 consist of $N = 26$ products and use a 20 - foot standard container. We randomly generate 50 instances for each test set, following similar procedures generating the MCLPP instances, so that the box assortment of generated SCLP instances is similar to the MCLPP instances. We should emphasize that SCLP instances are generated independently, which means the SCLP data are different from the MCLPP data.

We solve the 1 500 SCLP instances using the single container loading algorithm SCLP and set the time limit to $\tau = 2$ seconds per instance. We recorde the best solution found for each instance and reported the aggregated results in Table 4.3. For each test set in a class, we reporte two statistics: the average $u(t,N,\tau)$, and the standard deviation $s(t,N,\tau)$ of the results of 50 instances.

Table 4.3 Performance of the single container loading algorithm (SCLP), with the time limit per instance set to 2 seconds

Test Set by N	Class 20S		Class 40S		Class 40H	
	$u(t,N,2)$	$s(t,N,2)$	$u(t,N,2)$	$s(t,N,2)$	$u(t,N,2)$	$s(t,N,2)$
3	0.975	0.019	0.972	0.016	0.976	0.009
5	0.960	0.044	0.960	0.028	0.957	0.033
8	0.963	0.023	0.954	0.017	0.953	0.018
13	0.954	0.025	0.944	0.018	0.944	0.020
15	0.957	0.019	0.944	0.020	0.942	0.021
16	0.958	0.012	0.940	0.020	0.939	0.021
17	0.957	0.013	0.934	0.034	0.939	0.023
19	0.956	0.015	0.939	0.023	0.936	0.021
25	0.949	0.024	0.928	0.024	0.928	0.025
26	0.951	0.014	0.923	0.032	0.927	0.025

We repeate the experiment with the time limit per instance set to be 4, 8, and 16 seconds. The corresponding results are summarized in Tables 4.4, 4.5, and 4.6.

Table 4.4 Performance of the single container loading algorithm (SCLP), with the time limit per instance set to 4 seconds

Test Set by N	Class20S		Class40S		Class40H	
	$u(t,N,4)$	$s(t,N,4)$	$u(t,N,4)$	$s(t,N,4)$	$u(t,N,4)$	$s(t,N,4)$
3	0.977	0.019	0.974	0.015	0.978	0.009
5	0.962	0.044	0.962	0.029	0.960	0.034
8	0.964	0.024	0.959	0.015	0.957	0.017
13	0.957	0.026	0.951	0.016	0.954	0.016
15	0.960	0.019	0.953	0.015	0.951	0.017
16	0.962	0.011	0.948	0.017	0.950	0.017
17	0.961	0.013	0.945	0.025	0.949	0.018
19	0.959	0.015	0.948	0.018	0.945	0.019
25	0.953	0.023	0.937	0.021	0.936	0.022
26	0.955	0.012	0.933	0.025	0.934	0.025

Table 4.5 Performance of the single container loading algorithm (SCLP), with the time limit per instance set to 8 seconds

Test Set by N	Class20S		Class40S		Class40H	
	$u(t,N,8)$	$s(t,N,8)$	$u(t,N,8)$	$s(t,N,8)$	$u(t,N,8)$	$s(t,N,8)$
3	0.978	0.019	0.977	0.014	0.980	0.008
5	0.963	0.045	0.965	0.028	0.963	0.034
8	0.967	0.024	0.964	0.014	0.961	0.017
13	0.961	0.026	0.956	0.015	0.961	0.012
15	0.963	0.019	0.958	0.013	0.956	0.014
16	0.964	0.011	0.954	0.015	0.957	0.013
17	0.964	0.012	0.952	0.021	0.954	0.016
19	0.963	0.012	0.954	0.016	0.953	0.015
25	0.955	0.023	0.947	0.016	0.944	0.020
26	0.959	0.011	0.942	0.023	0.942	0.022

Table 4.6 Performance of the single container loading algorithm (SCLP), with the time limit per instance set to 16 seconds

Test Set by N	Class20S		Class40S		Class40H	
	$u(t,N,16)$	$s(t,N,16)$	$u(t,N,16)$	$s(t,N,16)$	$u(t,N,16)$	$s(t,N,16)$
3	0.979	0.019	0.978	0.013	0.982	0.008
5	0.964	0.045	0.967	0.029	0.964	0.034
8	0.970	0.021	0.967	0.014	0.965	0.015
13	0.963	0.026	0.960	0.014	0.963	0.012
15	0.966	0.014	0.960	0.013	0.960	0.013
16	0.966	0.011	0.958	0.014	0.960	0.012
17	0.966	0.012	0.956	0.019	0.957	0.015
19	0.965	0.012	0.957	0.014	0.955	0.015
25	0.960	0.015	0.951	0.015	0.949	0.018
26	0.961	0.010	0.947	0.019	0.949	0.018

A natural choice is to use the average as an estimation for a random SCLP instance appearing in the course of solving an MCLPP instance. For example, in an MCLPP instance with N products, if the time limit for solving an SCLP instance is set to τ, a type t container's usable volume will be estimated as:

$$U_t = u(t,N,\tau) \times L_t \times W_t \times H_t \tag{4.19}$$

We should point out that such estimation tends to underestimate the true capability of an SCLP algorithm on an MCLPP instance, due to the pooling effect presented below. In a typical MCLPP instance, a few containers are needed to load all products in an order, and low volume utilization of one container will usually be partially offset by high volume utilization of another. As a result, the average volume utilization tends to be higher than when we consider each container individually. We may partially address this issue by slightly adjusting our estimation upward:

$$U_t = \left(u(t,N,\tau) + \gamma \times s(t,N,\tau) \right) \times L_t \times W_t \times H_t \qquad (4.20)$$

We conduct computational experiments to help us decide whether we should set γ to 0 or 1.

4.6.3 Benefit of Employing Usable Volume

Recall that, in the first phase of our algorithm, we estimate unit shipping cost per preference for each row based on the usable volume of each container and rank all rows into ascending order based on the estimated unit shipping cost. We call this ranking the estimated ranking of rows.

If we set K in Algorithm 4 to be the size of R, we essentially force Algorithm 4.4 to consider all rows. For each row, we try to find the best solution in the row by solving a series of SCLP instances. We record the best solution for each row and rank the rows by best solution. This ranking is the actual ranking of rows.

If our estimated ranking is very similar to the actual ranking, we only need to consider the first few rows to find a good solution to the MCLPP, which will result in substantial savings of computing effort. Therefore, we can measure the effectiveness of our estimated usable volume by how similar the estimated ranking is to the actual ranking. Let e_r and a_r be the estimated and actual ranks of row r; then, we can measure the ranking distance by:

$$d^2 = \frac{\sum_{r \in R'} \left(e_r - a_r \right)^2}{|R'|} \qquad (4.21)$$

R' includes only those rows of R with cost $C \in \left[\underline{C}, \overline{C} \right]$. The smaller the distance, the more accurate the estimated ranking is with respect to the actual ranking. We can also use the estimated rank of the row with $a_r = 1$ as an indicator and denote it as e_{best}. For example, $e_{best} = 3$ means that the row containing the best solution is ranked as number 3 in our estimation. Clearly, a smaller value of e_{best} indicates a more accurate estimation. Note that setting K as e_{best} is sufficient for our MCLPP algorithm to return the best solution.

We use the following computational experiments to demonstrate the effectiveness of employing usable volume. We select the first five instances in each test set of class QBP to form a small test bed consisting of a total of 50 instances. We run three groups of experiments on the small test bed, using the following three settings for the usable volume of a type t container:

- Setting AVG+SD: $U_t = \left(u(t,N,\tau) + s(t,N,\tau)\right) \times L_t \times W_t \times H_t$
- Setting AVG: $U_t = u(t,N,\tau) \times L_t \times W_t \times H_t$
- Setting Naive UB: $U_t = L_t \times W_t \times H_t$ (i.e., all volume in a container can be fully utilized)

The two ranking accuracy indicators, d^2 and e_{best}, for each test instance are summarized in Table 4.7. The last row of the table reports the average for the 50 instances.

It is clear from Table 4.7 that, on average, either setting (i.e., AVG+SD or AVG) produces more accurate ranking than the setting Naive UB based on either indicator (i.e., d^2 or e_{best}).

Table 4.7 Accuracy of estimated row ranking under different settings

Test Set	Instance	AVG+SD		AVG		Naive UB	
		e_{best}	d^2	e_{best}	d^2	e_{best}	d^2
mclpp_3	1	1	3.294	1	2.111	1	2.706
mclpp_3	2	2	3.526	2	0.118	2	9.900
mclpp_3	3	1	4.061	2	5.040	1	29.515
mclpp_3	4	1	1.563	1	1.478	1	12.000
mclpp_3	5	1	0.267	3	8.333	1	6.938
mclpp_5	1	1	4.348	1	6.842	2	10.560
mclpp_5	2	1	4.818	1	11.263	2	16.870
mclpp_5	3	1	5.273	1	18.900	1	15.304
mclpp_5	4	2	6.750	1	5.500	2	11.538
mclpp_5	5	6	39.852	2	0.696	7	45.857
mclpp_8	1	1	4.148	1	24.000	2	29.613

续表

Test Set	Instance	AVG+SD		AVG		Naive UB	
		e_{best}	d^2	e_{best}	d^2	e_{best}	d^2
mclpp_8	2	1	3.000	1	21.250	2	36.129
mclpp_8	3	1	7.778	1	20.609	1	31.742
mclpp_8	4	1	1.576	2	22.759	5	76.919
mclpp_8	5	1	1.400	1	0.444	1	4.727
mclpp_13	1	1	0.000	1	0.333	1	0.222
mclpp_13	2	1	0.000	2	0.444	2	0.667
mclpp_13	3	1	0.250	1	0.750	1	0.667
mclpp_13	4	1	0.571	1	0.286	1	1.750
mclpp_13	5	1	0.000	1	0.000	1	2.000
mclpp_15	1	1	2.632	1	8.444	2	11.810
mclpp_15	2	4	23.895	1	12.333	5	28.870
mclpp_15	3	1	0.000	1	2.333	2	8.556
mclpp_15	4	1	1.143	1	0.923	1	6.353
mclpp_15	5	1	0.615	1	3.000	3	5.467
mclpp_16	1	2	4.167	1	6.476	4	30.429
mclpp_16	2	1	4.000	5	22.100	1	20.320
mclpp_16	3	1	1.478	1	8.400	1	19.704
mclpp_16	4	5	38.815	2	14.870	8	85.067
mclpp_16	5	2	2.625	1	5.130	8	39.158
mclpp_17	1	1	2.143	1	5.500	1	11.875
mclpp_17	2	1	1.429	4	6.000	1	5.467
mclpp_17	3	2	0.857	2	8.167	7	18.500
mclpp_17	4	1	0.462	1	8.727	5	17.500
mclpp_17	5	2	1.571	2	4.333	5	7.200
mclpp_19	1	1	1.200	1	0.500	1	1.333

续表

Test Set	Instance	AVG+SD		AVG		Naive UB	
		e_{best}	d^2	e_{best}	d^2	e_{best}	d^2
mclpp_19	2	1	0.800	2	0.400	1	5.333
mclpp_19	3	1	0.400	1	0.500	1	1.200
mclpp_19	4	3	4.800	1	0.500	5	8.667
mclpp_19	5	1	0.400	1	0.400	3	5.000
mclpp_25	1	2	4.390	1	26.973	6	79.837
mclpp_25	2	1	6.788	3	20.345	3	68.923
mclpp_25	3	5	18.538	6	49.182	1	54.625
mclpp_25	4	1	13.133	7	52.857	6	53.351
mclpp_25	5	1	3.677	6	21.333	9	79.730
mclpp_26	1	3	2.667	5	1.833	1	6.000
mclpp_26	2	1	1.818	2	0.400	5	2.615
mclpp_26	3	1	0.000	4	1.500	3	4.545
mclpp_26	4	2	57.520	2	57.520	15	117.243
mclpp_26	5	1	35.360	1	35.360	7	105.405
Average		1.560	6.596	1.900	10.750	3.160	25.114

The setting AVG+SD produces a more accurate ranking than the setting AVG, especially when the number of products is large (see test set QBP25 and QBP26). Therefore, we decide to use setting AVG + SD in all subsequent computational experiments.

4.6.4 Calibrate Parameters

The total execution time of our approach is determined primarily by two parameters: K, the number of rows to be explored in phase two, and τ, the time limit for solving one SCLP instance in the binary search in phase two.

We try to determine the best value for parameters through extensive computational experiments. We vary K from 1 to 10 and τ from 2^1 to 2^4

seconds. For each combination of K and τ, we execute our algorithm on each of the 50 instances in the small test bed introduced in Section 4.6.3.

For each instance, we record the total execution time and the unit shipping cost per preference corresponding to the best solution. For each pair of K and τ, we report the average execution time and the unit cost over 50 instances in a block in Table 4.8. The blocks are arranged by K into rows and by τ into column groups.

From Table 4.8, we see that, for each fixed τ, increasing K will lead to an improved solution when K is small. When K is large enough (say, $K>5$), further increasing K does not improve the overall solution. This is because, for the 50 instances, our estimated ranking of all rows is pretty close to the actual ranking. On the other hand, we know that we should consider at least two rows from our algorithm to reduce the chance of missing good solutions. In summary, we focus on $K=2$ to $K=5$ for this particular application environment.

Table 4.8 Average performance of our approach on test bed with various K and τ

K	2s		4s		8s		16s	
	time (s)	unit cost	time (s)	unit cost	time (s)	unit cost	time (s)	unit cost
1	0.887	28.822	1.852	28.478	3.444	28.381	6.388	28.245
2	1.770	28.774	3.511	28.458	6.978	28.345	13.166	28.227
3	2.788	28.688	5.343	28.444	10.436	28.202	19.968	28.075
4	3.738	28.623	7.267	28.321	13.707	28.177	27.294	28.075
5	4.721	28.558	9.059	28.314	17.090	28.177	33.690	28.075
6	5.518	28.557	10.673	28.307	20.824	28.177	39.915	28.075
7	6.385	28.557	12.276	28.307	24.244	28.177	45.764	28.075
8	7.137	28.557	14.075	28.307	27.539	28.177	51.766	28.075
9	8.140	28.557	15.581	28.307	30.583	28.177	56.328	28.075
10	8.928	28.557	17.126	28.307	33.415	28.177	61.899	28.075
Average	5.001	28.625	9.676	28.355	18.826	28.217	35.618	28.107

We can also observe the following simple trend in Table 4.8: The total execution time is roughly proportional to K for fixed τ and to τ for fixed K. That is, total time is given by $c \times K \times \tau$. It is, therefore, interesting to investigate the best allocation of K and τ when the total computation time is fixed.

For this purpose, we plot the same set of results in Figure 4.2. The horizontal axis gives the execution time (in the unit of 100 seconds), and the vertical axis gives the unit cost. Each point in the figure corresponds to the average result of 50 instances for a pair of K and τ. Points with the same τ are joined into a line. We can see that the best pair of K and τ depends on the total execution time. For example, if total execution time falls in the range of 1 300s to 1 400s, the pair ($K=4$, $\tau=8$) produces the best solution. However, if we reduce the total time to the range of 600s to 700s, the pair $K=1, \tau=16$ produces better results.

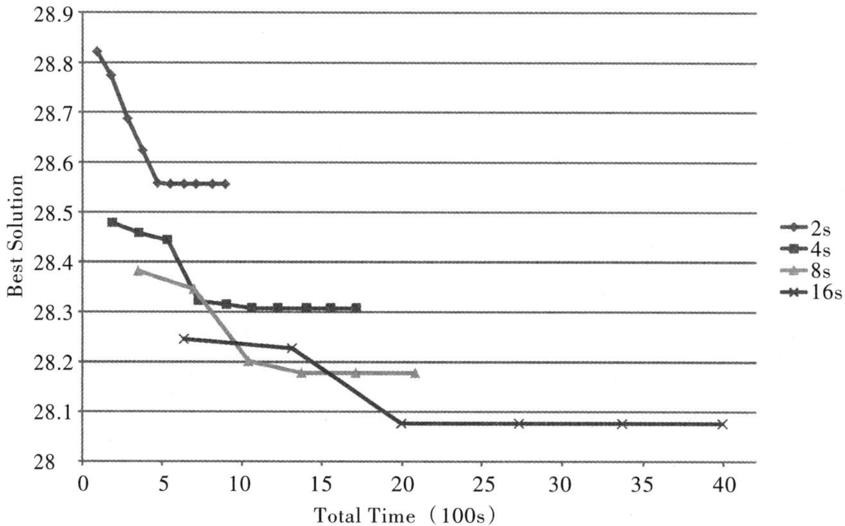

Figure 4.2 Average performance of our approach on test bed with various K and τ

In short, the best pair of K and τ depends on the total execution time available for each instance. In practice, we should calibrate the parameters based on historical data in a particular environment. For the benchmark data we generate, we decide to set the time limit per instance at about 700s;

therefore, we choose ($K=4, \tau=8$) to report our final results.

4.6.5 Computational Results

Table 4.9 summarizes the final results of our approach on the two classes of MCLPP instances with the following settings. We estimate the usable volume of a container based on $U_t = \left(u(t,N,\tau) + s(t,N,\tau)\right) \times L_t \times W_t \times H_t$ and set $K=4$, $\tau=8$. Each row in the table reports the average result over a set of 50 instances with the same number of product types N.

Detailed solution files and test data are available from our website, http://www.computational-logistics.org/orlib/MCLPP

Table 4.9 Average results of our approach on two classes of MCLPP instances

Test Set by N	Class QBP		Class VBP	
	time (s)	unit cost	time (s)	unit cost
3	1 371.840	5.051	1 360.060	5.143
5	1 259.960	10.206	1 358.820	10.999
8	952.240	15.556	935.800	16.058
13	807.280	28.697	763.500	30.897
15	697.400	30.128	677.960	33.126
16	1 044.840	30.907	1 042.540	33.945
17	1 128.800	35.283	1 105.220	37.480
19	1 308.520	36.896	1 247.000	39.974
25	903.500	48.905	898.300	55.484
26	930.520	48.920	931.520	53.287

4.7 Conclusion

We investigated the Multiple Container Loading Problem with Preference, inspired by the requirements of an international audio equipment manufacturer in Hong Kong. The manufacturer would like to help its customers reduce unit shipping costs by adjusting order quantity according to product preference. This problem was proved to be a generalized container loading problem with two item sets, where each set has mandatory items and optional items. However, the two item sets are not independent. Therefore, we proposed a new combinatorial formulation to capture the features of this problem. We then analyzed the solution space of our formulation and proposed an effective two-phase heuristic approach to solve the problem. In phase one of our approach, we estimate the most promising region of the solution space, based on performance statistics of the sub-problem solver—SCLP. In phase two, we find a feasible solution in the promising region by solving a series of 3D orthogonal packing problems.

We exploited the fact that most companies offer a relatively stable catalog of products and that most customer orders are also relatively stable. This enables us to better estimate the capability of the sub-routine (SCLP) based on statistical information regarding historical data. The high-level planning can take advantage of the estimation and search for better solutions in a short overall computing time.

A set of comprehensive test data were generated based on actual order data from one of our industrial partners. And we reported the solutions to the test instances found by our approach for further reference.

5 The Single Container Mix-Loading Problem

Manufacturers usually store their products in Palletized Storage Units (PSUs). PSUs are convenient for storage, but they are sometimes not cost effective for transportation because they can result in large empty spaces of waste in containers. To improve the utilization of its containers, a manufacturer is willing to remove products from PSUs (a process called *depalletizing*) and load the individual products, together with other PSUs, into a container. Once a PSU is depalletized, all of its products must be loaded into the container. No PSU can be depalletized if the total volume of complete PSUs loaded in the container is not maximized.

We introduce this problem as the Single Container Mix-Loading Problem (SCMLP) and prove that it is a generalized container loading problem. Then, we develop a two-phase constructive algorithm for the SCMLP that uses as the sub-routine a beam-search based method developed for loading items into a given set of spaces. In the first phase, the beam-search based method is called upon to load PSUs into the container. In the second phase, a proper set of PSUs is selected, and the beam-search based method is used to load all products of the selected PSUs into the remaining spaces in the container. The performance of our algorithm is demonstrated by experiments conducted on a set of instances generated from the historical data of the manufacturer.

5.1 Introduction

Manufacturers usually load their products onto pallets for storage. These loaded pallets are called Palletized Storage Units (PSUs) in industry. When delivering products, manufacturers load PSUs (instead of individual products) into containers (or trucks). Loading PSUs is convenient; however, large spaces on the tops or at the sides of the loaded PSUs could be wasted in each container. To improve the utilization of a container, an audio equipment manufacturer is willing to remove products from PSUs (a process called *depalletizing*) and load the products, together with other PSUs, into the container.

When a container delivered by the manufacturer arrives at its destination, all individual products loaded in it are rearranged into PSUs (a process called *repalletizing*). This is because moving PSUs from the port (or other unloading area) to the customer's warehouse is much more efficient and safe than moving individual products, and customers prefer to store PSUs rather than individual products in their warehouses. Therefore, once a PSU is depalletized, all of its products must be loaded into the container.

Both depalletizing and repalletizing increase the complexity of the manufacturer's operations, thus increasing its operational costs. Only when the transportation cost saved by improving the volume utilization of each container is much higher than the operational cost induced by depalletizing and repalletizing would the manufacturer prefer to depalletize PSUs and load products, together with PSUs, into containers. As a result, the partner manufacturer constrains that No PSU can be depalletized if the total volume of complete PSUs loaded in the container is not maximized.

To summarize, the audio equipment manufacturer would like to depalletize PSUs and load the individual products, together with other PSUs, into a container, such that the volume utilization of the container is maximized. Once a PSU is depalletized, all of its products must be loaded into the container. No PSU should be depalletized if the total volume of complete PSUs loaded in the container is not maximized. We name the resulting optimization problem the Single Container Mix-Loading Problem (SCMLP) and formally define it in Section 5.2.

In Section 5.3, we prove that the single container mix-loading problem is a generalized container loading problem. Then, we develop a two-phase constructive algorithm for the SCMLP, as described in Section 5.4. The algorithm uses a beam-search based method developed for loading items into a given set of spaces as a sub-routine. Beam search is a variant of the branch-and-bound technique, which expands the most promising nodes at each level of a search tree. In the first phase of our constructive algorithm, the beam-search based method is called upon to load PSUs into the container. In the second phase, a proper set of PSUs is selected, considering remaining volume of the container, and the beam-search based method is used to load all products of the selected PSUs into the remaining spaces of the container.

We generate 60 test instances based on historical data provided by the audio equipment manufacturer, and we conduct extensive computational experiments to demonstrate the effectiveness of our approach, as described in Section 5.5.

Commonly, the manufacturer's products are packaged in cuboid cartons. So, we use cartons to represent products in the following sections.

To the best of our knowledge, there is no literature concerned with the single container mix-loading problem. However, the SCMLP can be considered an extension of the Single Container Loading Problem (SCLP). When no PSU can be depalletized, the single container mix-loading problem is reduced to the single container loading problem.

5.2 Problem Definition

We are given a container denoted by C, whose dimensions are L, W, and H and whose volume is $V = LWH$, and a set of PSUs denoted by $\mathcal{P}$. Each PSU $p \in \mathcal{P}$ has the dimensions L_p, W_p and H_p and the volume $V_p = L_pW_pH_p$. We use an indicator d_p to denote whether PSU $p \in \mathcal{P}$ can be depalletized. If d_p equals 1, PSU p is depalletizable; otherwise, p is not depalletizable. Each PSU is composed of N_p identical cartons, and each carton in the PSU p has the dimensions l_p, w_p and h_p and the volume $v_p = l_pw_ph_p$. The set of all cartons in the PSU p is denoted by $\mathcal{J}_p$. It should be pointed out that the volume of a PSU may be larger than the total volume of the cartons contained within it ($V_p \geqslant N_pv_p$) because gaps between cartons may exist in each PSU.

We define a **depalletizable PSU set**, denoted by $\mathcal{D}$, as a set of PSUs ($\mathcal{D} \subseteq \mathcal{P}$) whose elements are all depalletizable ($d_p = 1, \forall p \in \mathcal{D}$), and we use the set $\mathcal{DP}$ to store all of the depalletizable PSU sets. Suppose there are n depalletizable PSUs in the set $\mathcal{P}$. In this case, the cardinality of the set $\mathcal{DP}$ is 2^n. Note that the empty set belongs to the set $\mathcal{DP}$.

As described in Section 5.1, in the single container mix-loading problem, we need to select two **disjoint** subsets of PSUs:

- $\mathcal{S}_1 \subseteq \mathcal{P}$: $\mathcal{S}_1$ is a set of complete PSUs.
- $\mathcal{S}_2 \subseteq \mathcal{DP}$: $\mathcal{S}_2$ is a depalletizable PSU set.

Next, we need to load all of the PSUs in $\mathcal{S}_1$ and all of the cartons in the set $\mathcal{J} = \bigcup_{p \in \mathcal{S}_2} \mathcal{J}_p$ into the container C, such that the total volume of the complete PSUs in the set $\mathcal{S}_1$ is maximized and the volume utilization of the container C is maximized. The volume utilization of the container C is defined as:

$$\frac{\sum_{p \in \mathcal{S}_1} V_p + \sum_{i \in \mathcal{I}} v_i}{V} \tag{5.1}$$

We define that a set of items, either PSUs or cartons, can be loaded into the container if the following constraints are satisfied:

- **Containment:** Each item must be placed completely within the container.
- **Orthogonal Placement:** Each item must be placed with its edges parallel to those of the container.
- **No Overlap:** Any two items inside the container do not overlap with each other.
- **Full Support:** The bottom of any item in the container must be fully supported by either the container floor or the tops of other items.
- **Orientation Restriction:** Every item must be placed in one of its allowed orientations. We use three flags (f^l, f^w, and f^h) to indicate whether an item can be placed with its length, width, and height, respectively, aligned with the vertical axis of the container.
  - For any pallet $p \in \mathcal{P}$, we have $f_p^l = 0$, $f_p^w = 0$, and $f_p^h = 1$.
  - For any carton $i \in \mathcal{I}_p, \forall p \in \mathcal{P}$, we have $f_i^l = 1$, $f_i^w = 1$, and $f_i^h = 1$.

5.3 The SCMLP is a Generalized Container Loading Problem

In the generalized container loading problem, we are given a set of three-dimensional containers denoted by $\mathcal{J}$. Each container $j \in \mathcal{J}$ has the cost C_j. Containers with the same dimensions and cost belong to the same type, and the types of containers are stored in the set $\mathcal{T}$. LB_t and UB_t denote the minimum and maximum number of containers of type $t \in \mathcal{T}$ that can be selected, and UB denotes the maximum number of containers of all types that can be used.

We are also given K sets of three-dimensional items. $\mathcal{I}_k$ is used to denote the k-th set of items, $\forall k = 1, \ldots, K$. Each item $i \in \mathcal{I}_k$ has the value v_i. Any set of items $\mathcal{I}_k$ can be divided into two subsets in this problem: the subset of mandatory items, denoted by $\mathcal{I}_k^M$, and the subset of optional items, denoted by $\mathcal{I}_k^O$, which equals $\mathcal{I}_k \backslash \mathcal{I}_k^M$.

We need to select one set of items and load all of its mandatory items, together with some or all of its optional items, into the limited number of container (s), such that the unit shipping cost is minimized. The unit shipping cost is defined as the quotient of the total cost of the selected containers and the total value of the loaded items.

The SCMLP can be proved to be a generalized container loading problem by considering that:

- Both $|\mathcal{J}|$ and $|\mathcal{T}|$ equal 1.
- The cost of the container equals its volume: $C_1 = V$.
- The limitation of container availability is defined as $UB_t = 1$, $LB_t = 1$, and $UB = 1$.
- The number of item sets (K) equals $|\mathcal{DP}|$. Sort elements in the set $\mathcal{DP}$, which consists of all depalletizable sets, in any order and denote the k-th element of $\mathcal{DP}$ as $\mathcal{D}_k$. Then, the item set $\mathcal{I}_k$ consists of the following two groups of items:
  - ◆ The group of mandatory items $\mathcal{I}_k^M$: all of the cartons depalletized from the PSUs in the depalletizable PSU set $\mathcal{D}_k$.
  - ◆ The group of optional items $\mathcal{I}_k^O$: all of the PSUs in the set $\mathcal{P} \backslash \mathcal{D}_k$.
- The value of a carton in the set $\mathcal{I}_k^M, k = 1, \cdots, K$ equals its volume.
- The value of a PSU $p \in \mathcal{I}_k^O, k = 1, \cdots, K$ is defined as αV_p, where V_p is the volume of p and α is a constant larger than 1.

The objective function of the generalized problem is to minimize the quotient of the volume of the container and the total volume of the loaded PSUs and cartons. This objective is equivalent to maximizing the volume utilization of the container. Since we define the value of a PSU to be larger than the total value of the cartons contained within it, a complete PSU will be favored over its individual cartons when loading the container. We can set a proper value to α, such that no PSU will be depalletized if the total volume of the complete PSUs loaded in the container is not maximized.

Suppose there are n depalletizable PSUs in the set $\mathcal{P}$. The cardinality of the set $\mathcal{DP}$ could be 2^n, that is to say, the number of item sets in the SCMLP (K) could be 2^n. Therefore, it is unrealistic to enumerate all item sets to find the optimal solution.

5.4 A Two-Phase Constructive Method

A two-phase constructive algorithm is developed for the SCMLP. It uses as its sub-routine a beam-search based method developed for loading items into a given set of spaces. Beam search is a variant of the branch-and-bound technique, which expands the most promising nodes at each level of a search tree. In the first phase of our constructive algorithm, the beam-search based method is called upon to load PSUs into the container. In the second phase, a proper set of PSUs is selected, considering remaining volume of the container, and the beam-search based method is used to load all products of the selected PSUs into the remaining spaces of the container.

Our constructive algorithm is a block building approach, according to the classification proposed by Pisinger [75]. In block building approaches, blocks of items, rather than individual items, are loaded into residual spaces.

5.4.1 A Beam-Search Based Method

Beam search is a tree search method whose search tree is built with a breadth-first strategy. However, in contrast to the breadth-first search, at each level of the search tree, only a predetermined number of nodes are selected by an evaluation function and expanded. This predetermined number is referred to as the beam width. If the beam width is infinite, all nodes will be selected and expanded at each level of the search tree; thus, the beam search is equivalent to the breadth-first search.

Each intermediate node of the search tree represents a partial solution to the problem, and each leaf node represents a complete solution. Beam search does not guarantee termination with an optimal solution because the nodes leading to the optimal solutions may be pruned.

We present a beam-search based method that iteratively calls upon a beam search in the following sections, solving problems in which we need to load three-dimensional items (e.g., PSUs and cartons in the SCMLP) into a given set of three-dimensional residual spaces in a container, such that the total volume of loaded items is maximized. It is a block building approach in which blocks of identical items, rather than individual items, are loaded into the residual spaces.

(1) Node Representation of Beam Search

Each node of the search tree of the beam search we developed is represented by four elements:

- A set of remaining items, denoted by I.
- A set of blocks, denoted by B.
- A set of three-dimensional residual spaces in the container C, denoted by R.
- A set of loaded items, denoted by LI.

A block $b \in B$ is the minimum bounding cuboid of an arrangement of items from the set I. The items in block b are identical, and they are arranged in such a way as to satisfy the orthogonal placement constraint, the no-overlap constraint, the full-support constraint, and the orientation restriction described in Section 5.2. We present the method for generating blocks in Section 5.4.1.

A residual space $r \in R$ is a fully-supported maximal space that does not overlap with any placed blocks in the container C. The *maximal space* concept was first introduced by Lim et al. [53] and has been used in several other works [40, 73, 90]. Figure 5.1 shows three new residual spaces generated when a block is placed in the the residual space r. We describe the generation approach for fully-supported maximal spaces in Section 5.4.1.

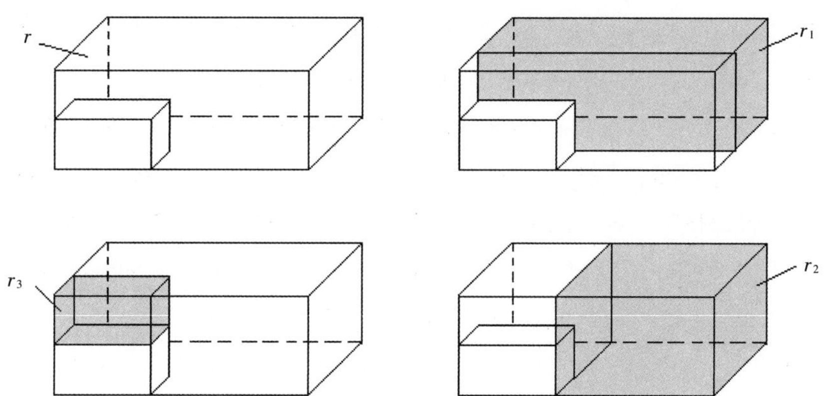

Figure 5.1 Three new residual spaces (r_1, r_2, r_3) generated when a block is placed in the residual space r

In the root node of the search tree, I contains all of the items given by the problem, B contains the blocks generated using the items in the set I, R contains all of the spaces given by the problem, and LI is empty. Each intermediate node of the search tree represents a partial solution to the problem, in which sets I, B, R, and LI are all non-empty. A leaf node represents a complete solution to the problem, in which I is an empty set, R is an empty set, or no item in I can be loaded into any space in R.

Block Generation:

In existing block building approaches for container loading problems, two types of blocks are generally used: namely, the simple block and the general block. A simple block consists of identical items, and all items in a simple block are placed with the same orientation. Therefore, each item in a simple block is fully supported from below by either the top of another item or the base of the block. A general block may either by composed of two or more types of items or be composed of identical items with different orientations. Special operations are involved in generating general blocks to satisfy the full-support constraint.

Both simple blocks and general blocks are proven to be effective when loading items into spaces [8, 20, 22, 56, 89, 90]. Zhu et al. [92] observed that using both simple blocks and general blocks is better for solving problems with strongly heterogeneous items, while using only simple blocks is better for solving problems with identical or weakly heterogeneous items. We use simple blocks in our beam-search based method because the full-support constraint is easily satisfied and because the PSUs and cartons in the SCMLP are weakly heterogeneous.

A simple block, made up of item $i \in I$, can be generated by replicating the item i for n_l, n_w, and n_h times along the length, width, and height, respectively, of the block. Therefore, all simple blocks composed of item i can be generated by enumerating all possible values of n_l, n_w, and n_h. Note that a single item i is also a simple block. The algorithm to generate simple blocks will be called upon only once at the beginning of the beam-search based method, and all the simple blocks form the set B of the root node of the search tree. Simple blocks with the same dimensions and containing the same set of items are considered to be duplicates, so only one of these is stored, and the others are deleted. Simple blocks that are too large to be loaded into any residual space in the root node are also deleted.

Residual Space Generation:

The residual spaces in the container C are fully-supported maximal spaces in our beam search. When no block is placed in a container, the whole space within the container is a fully-supported maximal space. Once a block is placed at a corner of the residual space r, three fully-supported maximal spaces are generated by: 1) performing a guillotine cut parallel to the length of r (see r_1 in Figure 5.1); 2) performing a guillotine cut parallel to the width of r (see r_2 in Figure 5.1); and 3) cutting a space above the block, such that the base of the space is the top of the block (see r_3 in Figure 5.1). Note that the spaces r_1 and r_2 in Figure 5.1 overlap with each other.

Due to overlapping between fully-supported maximal spaces, when a block is placed at a corner of a residual space, it may intrude into other residual spaces. Figure 5.2 shows an example in which a block b is placed in the residual space r_1 and intrudes into the residual space r_2.

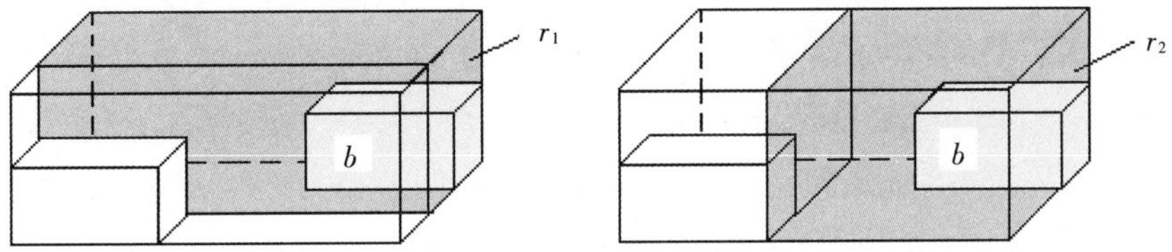

Figure 5.2 A block b intrudes into the residual space r_2 when it is placed in the residual space r_1.

Once a block b is placed in a residual space, the intruded residual spaces must be updated as follows. We first perform, at most, two guillotine cuts parallel to the length of r, which will result in two fully-supported maximal spaces (see r_2 and r_4 in Figure 5.3). Next, we perform, at most, two guillotine cuts parallel to the width of r, which will result in two fully-supported maximal spaces (see r_1 and r_3 in Figure 5.3). Finally, we cut a space above the block, such that the base of the space is the top of the block (see r_5 in Figure 5.3). No space below the block will be generated because of the full-support constraint. Therefore, we will get, at most, five fully-supported maximal spaces when updating an intruded residual space. Figure 5.3 demonstrates the five new residual spaces generated when a block b intrudes into the residual space r.

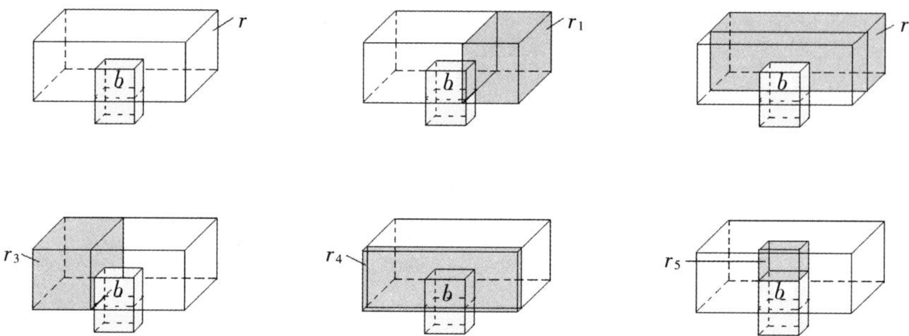

Figure 5.3 Five new residual spaces (r_1, r_2, r_3, r_4, and r_5) generated when a block b intrudes into the residual space r.

(2) Child Node Generation of Beam Search

Consider an intermediate node whose elements are I, B, R, and LI. We call this a parent node. One child of the parent node is generated by placing a block $b \in B$ into a residual space $r \in R$.

Space Selection:

Each residual space is a cuboid and has eight corners. Each corner of the residual space r is associated with a corner of the container C (see Figure 5.4). For example, the front-left-bottom corner of r is related to the front-left-bottom corner of C. The Manhattan distance between a corner of the residual space r and the corresponding corner of the container C is defined as $|x_1 - x_2| + |y_1 - y_2| + |z_1 - z_2|$, where (x_1, y_1, z_1) is the coordinate of the corner of r and (x_2, y_2, z_2) is the coordinate of the corner of C (see Figure 5.4). The corner of r with the smallest Manhattan distance from its corresponding corner of C is called the *anchor corner*, and the smallest Manhattan distance is called the *anchor distance*.

When generating a child of an intermediate node, the beam search selects the usable residual space of R with the smallest anchor distance. Ties are broken by larger volume. A usable residual space is a residual space that is large enough to accommodate at least one block of B.

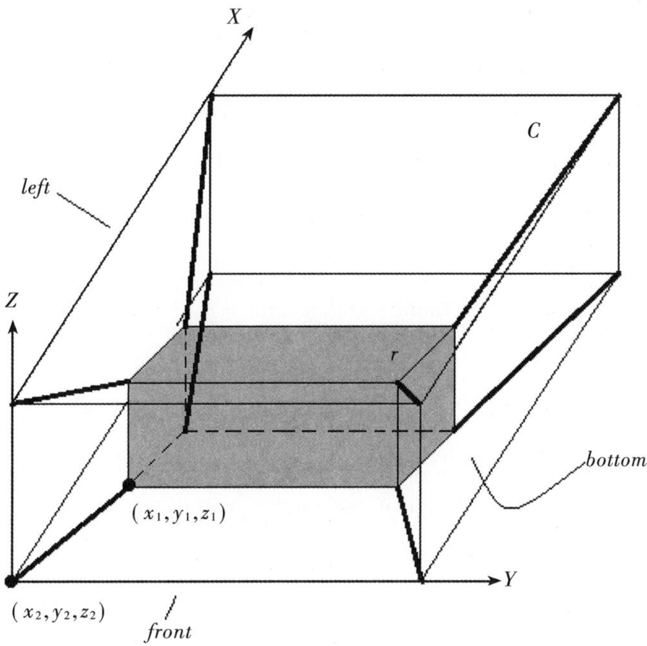

Figure 5.4 The relationship between the corners of the residual space r and the corners of the container C

Block Selection:

Given the selected residual space $r \in R$, we use function $f(b,r) = V - (V_{waste} - V_{loss})$ to evaluate each block $b \in B$. The block with the largest value of $f(b,r)$ is selected. This function was introduced by Zhu et al. [90]. V is the total volume of all the items in block b. V_{waste} is the difference between the volume of block b and V. V_{loss} is the lower bound of the unusable volume of the residual space r. The unusable volume of the residual space r is the difference between the volume of r and the maximum total volume of items in I that can be loaded into r.

If the block b cannot be loaded into the residual space r, the function $f(b,r)$ returns negative infinity; otherwise, V_{loss} is computed as follows. We first calculate the remaining length (width, height) of the residual space r that can be used after placing the block b and denote this length (width, height) by l (w, h). Next, we find the dimensions of each item $i \in I$ that can be placed along the length (width, height) of the residual space r and store all these dimensions in the set L_r (W_r, H_r). Then, we solve the knapsack problem, in which the capacity of the knapsack is l (w, h) and the set of items to be packed in the knapsack is L_r (W_r, H_r), using the standard Dynamic Programming (DP) algorithm proposed by Martello and Toth [57] which runs in pseudo-polynomial time. Suppose the optimal solution value returned by the dynamic programming algorithm is l_{max} (w_{max}, h_{max}). In this case, V_{loss} is equal to $V(r)-(l(b)+l_{max})\times(w(b)+w_{max})\times(h(b)+h_{max})$, where $V(r)$ is the volume of the residual space r and $l(b)$, $w(b)$, and $h(b)$ are the length, width, and height, respectively, of the block b.

Once the block b is placed at the anchor corner of the selected residual space r, all four elements of the parent node (I, B, R, and LI) are updated. The updated elements are inherited by the child node generated by placing b in r.

Updating the Item Set I, the Block Set B, and the Loaded-Item Set LI:

The block b placed in the residual space r will be deleted from B, and all items contained in b will be deleted from I and inserted into LI. Some blocks in B are also deleted because there are not enough items in I to form these blocks.

Updating the Residual-Space Set R:

Once the block b is placed in the residual space r, new residual spaces will be generated according to the method described in Section 5.4.1. The residual space r will be deleted from the set R, and all newly generated residual spaces will be inserted into R. Due to the overlapping nature of the fully-supported maximal spaces, some spaces may be completely contained by other residual spaces. Therefore, a process is called upon to delete these completely contained residual spaces once new residual spaces are inserted into R. There are also spaces that are too small to accommodate any block in the updated block set B. These small residual spaces are marked as unusable, but they are not deleted from R.

(3) Node Evaluation of Beam Search

In beam search, at each level of the search tree, only a number (beam width) of child nodes are selected for further expansion, based on an evaluation approach. In our beam search, we use a greedy strategy to construct a complete solution from a given child node and use the total volume of loaded items in the complete solution to evaluate the child node.

The greedy strategy works as follows. Given a child node (I, B, R, LI) representing a partial solution to the SCMLP, a complete solution (I', B', R', LI') is constructed by iteratively calling upon the four operations:

- Select the usable residual space $r \in R$ with the minimum anchor distance.
- Select the block $b \in B$ with the maximum value of the function $f(b, r)$.
- Place the selected block b in the selected residual space r.
- Update the item set, the block set, the residual-space set, and the loaded-item set into I', B', R', and LI'.

This continues until there is no item remaining in I', there is no usable residual space remaining in R', or no item can be loaded into any usable residual space. Then, the evaluation function of the given child node is the total volume of loaded items in the corresponding complete solution, which is denoted by $g(LI')$.

(4) The Beam-Search Based Method

Our beam-search based method is described in Algorithm 5.1, which iteratively calls upon the beam search presented in Algorithm 5.2.

Algorithm 5.1 The Beam-Search Based Method

```
BSM (I,R,LI)
   // Input: I:  a set of items
   //        R:  a set of residual spaces
   //        LI: a set of loaded items
bestSol = NULL
w = 1
B = generate all simple blocks composed in I
while time limit is not exceeded
        bestSol = BeamSearch (I,B,R,LI)
        w = ⌈√2 w⌉
return bestSol
```

The input of the beam-search based method includes a set of three-dimensional items I and a set of three-dimensional residual spaces R, both given by the problem. *bestsol* is used to store the best complete solution found by the method, and it consists of four elements, I_{best}, B_{best}, R_{best}, and LI_{best}, which represent the set of remaining items, the set of blocks composed of items in I_{best}, the set of remaining residual spaces, and the set of loaded items, respectively. The beam width of our beam search is represented by the parameter w. w also determines the search effort because it limits the number of child nodes that can be generated and evaluated to be, at most, w^2, as presented in Algorithm 5.2. w is increased to $\lceil \sqrt{2}w \rceil$ after each execution of Algorithm 5.2, such that the search effort is doubled.

The beam search iteratively called upon in our beam-search based method is described in Algorithm 5.2.

Algorithm 5.2 Beam Search

```
BeamSearch (I,B,R,LI)
    // Input: I: a set of items
    //   B: a set of blocks each of which consists of items in I
    //   R: a set of residual spaces
    //   LI: a set of loaded items
bestSol = NULL
n0 = root node (I,B,R,LI)
N = {n0}
while N ≠ ϕ
    the set of child nodes N' = ϕ
    for ni = (Ii,Bi,Ri,LIi) ∈ N
        if ni = n0
            Children = GeneratedChildNodes (I,B,R,LI,w²)
        else
            Children = GeneratedChildNodes (I,B,R,LI,w)
        N' = N' ∪ Children
    (bestChildren,bestSol) = Greedy (w,N',bestSol)
    N = bestChildren
return bestSol
```

The root node is initialized with the four elements I, B, R, and LI. A set N is used to store all of the nodes at the current level of the search tree. Each iteration in Algorithm 5.2 executes the following operations: 1) w child nodes of each node $n_i \in N$ are generated using Algorithm 5.3, and all w^2 child nodes are stored in set N'; 2) only w nodes in set N' are selected to compose the next level of the search tree using Algorithm 8. Note that w^2 child nodes will be generated for the root node, such that each level of the search tree has the same number of children [1]. *bestSol* stores the best complete solution found by Algorithm 5.4.

The method for generating w child nodes of a given node (I_i, B_i, R_i, LI_i) is presented in Algorithm 5.3.

Algorithm 5.3 Generate w Child Nodes of Node (I_i, B_i, R_i, LI_i)

GenerateChildNodes (I_i, B_i, R_i, LI_i, w)
// **Input**: I_i: a set of items
// B_i: a set of blocks each of which consists of items in set I_i
// R_i: a set of residual spaces
// LI_i: a set of loaded items
// w: the number of child nodes to be generated
children = ϕ
select the residual space $r \in R_i$ with the minimum anchor distance
if $w > |B_i|$
  $B = B_i$
else
  B = the w blocks in B_i that maximize $f(b, r)$
for $b \in B_i$
  place b at the anchor corner of r
  I_i' = update I_i, B_i' = update B_i, R_i' = update R_i, LI_i' = update LI_i
  put the *child* = $(I_i', B_i', R_i', LI_i')$ into *children*
return *children*

A residual space $r \in R_i$ with the minimum anchor distance is selected, with details described in Section 5.4.1. Blocks in B_i are ranked into descending order based on the value of $f(b, r)$ (see Section 5.4.1) and the first w blocks in the rank are selected. If the number of available blocks in B_i is smaller than w, all of the blocks in B_i are selected. Then, at most w child nodes of (I_i, B_i, R_i, LI_i) are generated by placing each selected block at the anchor corner of the selected residual space r.

Algorithm 5.4 describes the method for selecting w nodes from the set of child nodes of the current level of the search tree (N'). For each child node $n_i = (I_i, B_i, R_i, LI_i) \in N'$, we iteratively call upon Algorithm 5.3 with $w = 1$ until all items in I_i are loaded, all residual spaces in R_i are occupied, or no item in I_i can be loaded into any residual space in R_i. The resultant node is a leaf node $leaf_i = (I_i', B_i', R_i', LI_i')$ representing a complete solution, and it is evaluated using the function $g(LI_i')$ (see Section 5.4.1). Then, we rank all the nodes $n_i = N'$ into descending order based on the value of $g(LI_i')$ and select the first w nodes in the rank. Since each leaf node corresponds to a complete solution, we update the best solution *bestSol* with the first node in the ranking, if necessary. Note that, if the cardinality of N' is smaller than w, all nodes of N' are selected.

Algorithm 5.4 Select *w* Best Nodes Using a Greedy Strategy

```
Greedy (w, N', bestSol)
  // Input: w: the number of nodes to be selected
  //        N': a set of nodes
  //        bestSol: the best solution found so far
leafPool = ϕ, bestChildren = ϕ
if w > |N'|
    return (N', bestSol)
else
  for n_i = (I_i, B_i, R_i, LI_i) ∈ N'
      I = I_i, B = B_i, R = R_i, LI = LI_i
      while I ≠ ϕ and R ≠ ϕ and some item in I can be placed in a residual space r ∈ R
          leaf_i = (I_i', B_i', R_i', LI_i') = GenerateChildrenNodes(I, B, R, LI, 1)
          I = I_i', B = B_i', R = R_i', LI = LI_i'
      put leaf_i in leafPool
  bestChildren = the w nodes in N' whose leafs have the maximum g(LI')
  if bestSol = ϕ
      bestSol = leaf in leafPool with maximum g(LI')
  else
      if the maximum g(LI') of leafPool < g(LI_best)
          bestSol = leaf in leafPool with maximum g(LI')
return (bestChildren, bestSol)
```

5.4.2 The Two-Phase Constructive Algorithm

We develop a two-phase constructive algorithm for the single container mix-loading problem, which is described in Algorithm 5.5.

Algorithm 5.5 The Two-Phase Constructive Method

```
TwoPhase (𝒫, 𝒞)
   // Input: 𝒫: a set of PSUs
   //        C: the container
sol = NULL
I = all of the PSUs in 𝒫
R = C
solP1 = (I_solP1, B_solP1, R_solP1, LI_solP1) = BSM(I, R, ϕ)
if I_solP1 = ϕ or R_solP1 = ϕ
  return solP1
else
   D = all of the depalletizable PSUs in I_solP1
   R = R_solP1, LI = LI_solP1
   V_R = the total volume of all of the residual spaces in R
   if V_R < the smallest V_p, ∀p ∈ D
      return solP1
   else
      lb = 0, ub = 1, factory = 0
      while ub − lb > 0.01
         I* = D, R* = R, LI* = LI
         factor = (ub + lb) / 2
         I′ = solve SelectCartons (V_R, I*, factor)
         tempSol = (I_t, B_t, R_t, LI_t) = BSM(I′, R*, LI*)
         tempSol = (I_t ∪ I_solP1\D, B_t, R_t, LI_t )
         if I_t = ϕ
           lb = factor
           solP2 = (I_solP2, B_solP2, R_solP2, LI_solP2) = tempSol
         else
            ub = factor
return solP2
```

The inputs of the algorithm are the given set of PSUs ($\mathcal{P}$) and the given container (C). In the first phase of our constructive algorithm, the beam-search based method (Algorithm 5.1) is called upon to load PSUs in $\mathcal{P}$ into the given container C, such that the total volume of loaded complete PSUs is maximized. At the end of the first phase, if all of the given PSUs are loaded into the container, or if there is no residual space in the container, the algorithm returns the solution found in the first phase ($solP1$) and terminates; otherwise, the algorithm continues with the second phase. Note that all the unusable residual spaces generated during the beam search are not deleted (see Section 5.4.1), so no residual space existing in the container means that no usable or unusable residual space exists in the container.

In the second phase of the algorithm, we first store all the depalletizable PSUs that are not loaded into the container in the set I and store all the residual spaces in the container in the set R; meanwhile, we mark all the unusable residual spaces in R as usable. Suppose the total volume of all the residual spaces in R is V_R. If V_R is smaller than the smallest depalletizable PSU in I, no PSU in I can be loaded into any residual space in R; therefore, the algorithm returns the solution $solP1$ and terminates; otherwise, the second phase continues with a binary search.

The binary search is used to determine the maximum volume of PSUs whose cartons can be loaded into the residual spaces in R. In each iteration of the binary search, first, Algorithm 5.6 is called upon to solve the integer programming problem **SC** and depalletize all the PSUs, which are selected by solving **SC**, into cartons.

$$\mathbf{SC}(V_R, D, factor): \text{Maximize} \sum_{p \in D} V_p x_p \tag{5.2}$$

Subject to

$$\sum_{p \in D} V_p x_p \leqslant factor \times V_R \tag{5.3}$$

$$x_p \in \{0,1\}, \forall p \in D \tag{5.4}$$

Algorithm 5.6 **Select PSUs in I^* and Depalletize Then into Cartons**

```
SelectCartons (V_R, I*, factor)
   // Input: V_R: the total volume of a set of residual spaces
   //       I*: a set of PSUs
   //       factor: a parameter
I_cartons = φ
I = solve the problem SC (V_R, I*, factor) using CPLEX
I_cartons = all of the cartons depalletized from PSUs in I
return I_cartons
```

Next, the beam-search based method is used again to load cartons selected by Algorithm 5.6 into the residual spaces in R. If all the cartons can be loaded into the residual spaces in R, the current best solution to the single container mix-loading problem (*tempSol*) is generated, and we increase *lb* of the binary search in the expectation of finding a better solution; otherwise, we decrease *ub* of the binary search to increase the chance that the newly depalletized cartons can be totally loaded into the residual spaces in R.

5.5 Computational Experiments

Our two-phase constructive algorithm was implemented as a sequential algorithm in Java (JDK 7 updated 21, 64-bit edition), and no multi-threading was explicitly used. All experiments described in this section were conducted on a personal computer equipped with an Intel Core (TM) i7-3770 CPU clocked at 3.40 gigahertz with 8 gigabyte of RAM, running a Windows 7 (64-bit) operating system. The commercial integer linear programming solver used was the IBM ILog CPLEX Optimization Studio 12.2 (64-bit) with its default settings.

Since there is no standard benchmark data for the single container mix-loading problem, we generated 60 SCMLP instances based on historical data provided by the audio equipment manufacturer to test the effectiveness of our approach. The details are presented in Section 5.5.1. The beam-search based method we described in Section 5.4.1 can be used to solve the single container loading problem, therefore, we test the beam-search based method on the well-known SCLP benchmark instances and report its performance in Section 5.5.2. We demonstrate the performance of the two-phase constructive algorithm for all SCMLP instances in Section 5.5.3.

5.5.1 Generate Test Instances

We collected 12-month purchase order data from an audio equipment manufacturer in Hong Kong. Most orders consist of N types of PSUs, with N coming from the set {1, 2, 3, 4, 5, 6}. Each PSU contains identical products packaged in cartons. Information about each PSU is provided, including the dimensions of the PSU, the dimensions of the cartons in the PSU, and the number of the cartons in the PSU. The 40-foot standard container, with dimensions of 12 045 mm by 2 309 mm by 2 379 mm, is used for each order.

We generate 60 SCMLP instances, of which 7 instances have one type of PSU, 14 instances have two types of PSUs, 12 instances have three types of PSUs, 14 instances have four types of PSUs, 7 instances have five types of PSUs, and 6 instances have six types of PSUs.

Each instance is generated as follows. We first set a target V for the total volume of PSUs in the instance. The target volume is randomly generated so that it is larger than the volume of the 40-foot standard container. We then uniformly randomly select N types of PSUs from the orders provided by the manufacturer and initialize their quantities to 1. Next, we uniformly randomly select one type from the N types of PSUs and increase its quantity by 1. We repeatedly increase the quantity of each type of PSU until the total volume of all PSUs in the instance exceeds the target volume V. The manufacturer did not provide information regarding which PSUs are depalletizable; therefore, we randomly set some types of PSUs in the instance to be depalletizable. Furthermore, we suppose that each PSU in the instance can only be rotated along its height, but that any carton contained in the PSU is fully rotatable.

5.5.2 Computational Results

We set the time limit for beam search to be 500 seconds and perform the two - phase constructive algorithm on the 60 SCMLP instances. Table 5.2 summarizes the final results. Each row in the table reports the instance, the number of PSU types involved in the instance, the volume utilization of the solution found in the first phase of the algorithm ($Util_1$), the volume utilization of the final solution found by the algorithm ($Util_2$), and the number of PSUs that are depalletized in the final solution. Note that, in the solution found in the first phase of the constructive algorithm, only complete PSUs are loaded into the container.

The results in Table 5.1 show that the volume utilization is increased by approximately 3% by packing cartons into the container.

Table 5.1 Results of performing the two-phase constructive algorithm on the 60 test instances

Instance	PSU Type #	$Util_1$ (%)	$Util_1$ (%)	Depalletized PSUs #
1	1	83.57373	85.98562	2
2	1	77.63049	80.81452	4
3	1	69.44609	71.83724	2
4	1	61.33801	63.88265	2
5	1	61.11359	63.43719	2
6	1	56.97283	59.3111	2
7	1	88.58754	90.99943	2
8	2	77.69688	80.51763	3
9	2	74.83335	77.64884	2
10	2	86.7961	89.34074	2
11	2	83.57373	86.39959	2

续表

Instance	PSU Type #	$Util_1$（%）	$Util_1$（%）	Depalletized PSUs #
12	2	89.28748	92.11393	2
13	2	84.3093	87.49334	4
14	2	90.72358	93.90762	4
15	2	68.4428	68.4428	0
16	2	75.47155	78.67583	3
17	2	84.3093	86.78972	2
18	2	64.6537	67.47343	2
19	2	78.46042	81.22785	2
20	2	79.27384	80.89375	1
21	2	82.49789	85.51195	2
22	3	83.7379	86.56375	2
23	3	83.9237	86.54548	2
24	3	88.17368	90.72965	2
25	3	84.3093	87.49334	4
26	3	79.01022	81.90744	3
27	3	82.71829	82.71829	0
28	3	74.93958	77.35139	2
29	3	69.22	72.03973	2
30	3	83.77385	86.48682	2
31	3	79.35866	82.18511	2
32	3	83.61702	83.61702	0
33	3	69.44609	72.27254	2
34	4	89.39198	92.28233	2
35	4	91.56617	94.75194	3
36	4	81.96477	84.95188	3
37	4	82.83163	85.84569	2
38	4	91.05366	94.12973	3
39	4	90.42722	93.58719	3
40	4	91.87938	94.57942	2

续表

Instance	PSU Type #	$Util_1$（%）	$Util_1$（%）	Depalletized PSUs #
41	4	90.11682	93.24376	2
42	4	84.81748	87.71469	3
43	4	89.33439	92.40148	2
44	4	87.74436	90.90223	2
45	4	85.14837	88.33241	4
46	4	87.40939	90.23013	3
47	4	84.42069	87.31076	2
48	5	91.37458	94.58887	3
49	5	91.29549	94.47953	4
50	5	89.78696	92.86304	3
51	5	85.53575	88.54981	2
52	5	85.00928	87.55392	2
53	5	86.6137	89.3145	2
54	5	76.65078	79.47051	2
55	6	88.51699	91.73128	3
56	6	88.0429	91.25719	3
57	6	92.98708	96.11402	2
58	6	86.65769	89.67175	2
59	6	84.55776	87.24833	2
60	6	89.7981	93.00619	3

5.6 Conclusion

We investigated the Single Container Mix-Loading Problem, which was inspired by the requirements of an international audio equipment manufacturer in Hong Kong. The manufacturer stores its products in Palletized Storage Units（PSUs). When delivering products, loading PSUs, rather than individual products, into containers（or trucks）is convenient;

however, large spaces in each container could be wasted. To improve the utilization of a container, the manufacturer is willing to depalletize PSUs and load the individual products, together with other PSUs, into a container. Once a PSU is depalletized, all of its products must be loaded into the container, and no PSU can be depalletized if the total volume of complete PSUs loaded in the container is not maximized.

We proved that the single container mix-loading problem is a generalized container loading problem. Then, we develop a two-phase constructive algorithm for the SCMLP. The algorithm uses as its sub-routine a beam-search based method, which iteratively calls upon a beam search. In the first phase of our constructive algorithm, the beam-search based method is called upon to load complete PSUs into the container. In the second phase, a proper set of PSUs is selected considering the remaining volume of the container, and the beam-search based method is used to load all products depalletized from the selected PSUs into the remaining spaces of the container.

We generated 60 test instances, based on historical data provided by the audio equipment manufacturer, and we reported the solutions to the test instances found by the two-phase constructive algorithm for further reference.

6 Conclusion

In this book, we introduced the generalized container loading problem to model a more practical container loading issue. In this problem, we are given a set of three-dimensional containers and several sets of three-dimensional items. Each set of items can be further divided into two groups: mandatory items and optional items. Each container is characterized by its dimensions and cost, while each item is characterized by its dimensions and value. We need to select one set of items and load some or no optional items, together with all the set's mandatory items, into the container(s), such that the unit shipping cost is minimized. The unit shipping cost is defined as the result of dividing the total cost of the selected containers by the total value of the loaded items.

The generalized container loading problem describes some common issues in the modern freight transportation and logistics industry, which have not received enough attention in existing literature. The contribution of the generalized container loading problem is two-fold. First, this problem describes a multilayer decision - making process, which is a difficulty frequently encountered by decision makers. The decisions include: (1) which set of items to choose; (2) which optional items of the selected item set should be loaded together with the mandatory ones; (3) which container combination should be used to accommodate all selected items. Second, this problem jointly considers container cost, item value, and practical constraints in container loading problems. In particular, the generalized container loading problem can handle different unit settings for container cost and item value.

We presented two mathematical models to capture the features of the generalized container loading problem. One is a mixed-integer programming model, which describes, in detail, the assignment and placement of items in containers. The other model is a set-covering model, which hides the loading details and dramatically increases computational efficiency.

A number of classic container loading problems were proved to be special cases of the generalized container loading problem, including the single container loading problem, the three-dimensional bin packing problem, the three-dimensional variable-sized bin packing problem, and the multiple container loading cost minimization problem.

Two applications of the generalized container loading problem were demonstrated in this book. Both of them are real issues encountered by manufacturers in their logistics processes.

In the first application, we investigated the Multiple Container Loading Problem with Preference, inspired by the requirements of an international audio equipment manufacturer in Hong Kong. The manufacturer would like to help its customers reduce unit shipping costs by adjusting order quantity according to product preference. This problem was proved to be a generalized container loading problem with two item sets, where each set has mandatory items and optional items. However, the two item sets are not independent. Therefore, we proposed a new combinatorial formulation to capture the features of this problem. We then analyzed the solution space of our formulation and proposed an effective two-phase heuristic approach to solve the problem. In phase one of our approach, we estimate the most promising region of the solution space, based on performance statistics of the sub-problem solver - SCLP. In phase two, we find a feasible solution in the promising region by solving a series of 3D orthogonal packing problems.

We exploited the fact that most companies offer a relatively stable catalog of products and that most customer orders are also relatively stable. This enables us to better estimate the capability of the sub-routine (SCLP) based on statistical information regarding historical data. The high-level planning can take advantage of the estimation and search for better solutions in a short overall computing time.

A set of comprehensive test data were generated based on actual order data from one of our industrial partners. And we reported the solutions to the test instances found by our approach for further reference.

In the second application, we investigated the Single Container Mix-Loading Problem, which was inspired by the requirements of an international audio equipment manufacturer in Hong Kong. The manufacturer stores its products in Palletized Storage Units (PSUs). When delivering products, loading PSUs, rather than individual products, into containers (or trucks) is convenient; however, large spaces in each container could be wasted. To improve the utilization of a container, the manufacturer is willing to depalletize PSUs and load the individual products, together with other PSUs, into a container. Once a PSU is depalletized, all of its products must be loaded into the container, and no PSU can be depalletized if the total volume of complete PSUs loaded in the container is not maximized.

We proved that the single container mix-loading problem is a generalized container loading problem. Then, we develop a two-phase constructive algorithm for the SCMLP. The algorithm uses as its sub-routine a beam-search based method, which iteratively calles upon a beam search. In the first phase of our constructive algorithm, the beam-search based method is called upon to load complete PSUs into the container. In the second phase, a proper set of PSUs is selected considering the remaining volume of the container, and the beam-search based method is used to load all products depalletized from the selected PSUs into the remaining spaces of the container.

We generated 60 test instances, based on historical data provided by the audio equipment manufacturer, and we reported the solutions to the test instances found by the two-phase constructive algorithm for further reference.

In the future, we may exploit more practical container loading problems that can be proved to be the generalized container loading problem. Since the generalized container loading problem is NP-hard to the strong sense, heuristic methods will dominate other methods in future research on solving this problem. Generally, the performance of a heuristic method developed for an optimization problem is evaluated by its performance on benchmark test instances of the problem. However, this evaluation may be biased because the test instances do not estimate characteristics of the whole population of the instances of the problem. Therefore, we need to device new methods to evaluate a heuristic method. Another direction of our research is developing lower bounds and upper bounds for the generalized container loading problem based on the general model we proposed. Both lower bounds and upper bounds are helpful for evaluating the quality of the solutions found by algorithms developed for the generalized container loading problem. The lower bounds and upper bounds are also the foundation of developing advanced solution methods, such as the branch-and-bound based methods, the branch-and-cut based methods, and the column-generation based method.

Bibliography

[1] ARAYA I, RIFF M C. A beam search approach to the container loading problem [J]. Computers & Operations Research, 2014, 43: 100–107.

[2] BANSAL N, HAN X, IWAMA K, et al. Harmonic algorithm for 3-dimensional strip packing problem: proceedings of the Eighteenth Annual ACM-SIAM Symposium on Discrete Algorithm, New Orleans, Louisiana, January 07–09, 2007 [C]. New York: ACM Press, 2007.

[3] BISCHOFF E. Three-dimensional packing of items with limited load bearing strength [J]. European Journal of Operational Research, 2006, 168(3): 952–966..

[4] BISCHOFF E, RATCLIFF M. Issues in the development of approaches to container loading [J]. The International Journal of Management Science, 1995, 23(4): 377–390.

[5] BISCHOFF E, JANETZ F, RATCLIFF M. Loading pallets with non-identical items [J]. European Journal of Operational Research, 1995, 84(3): 681–692.

[6] BISCHOFF E, MARRIOTT M D. A comparative evaluation of heuristics for container loading [J]. European Journal of Operational Research, 1990, 44(2): 267–276.

[7] BORTFELDT A, GEHRING H. A hybrid genetic algorithm for the container loading problem [J]. European Journal of Operational Research, 2001, 131(1): 43–61.

[8] BORTFELDT A, GEHRING H, MACK D. A parallel tabu search algorithm for solving the container loading problem [J]. Parallel Computing, 2003, 29(5): 641–662.

[9] BRUNETTA L, GREGOIRE P. A general purpose algorithm for three-dimensional packing [J]. INFORMS Journal on Computing, 2005, 17(3): 328–338.

[10] CESCHIA S, SCHAERF A. Local search for a multi-drop multi-container loading problem [J]. Journal of Heuristics, 2011, 19(2): 275–294.

[11] CHE C H, HUANG W, LIM A, ZHU W. The multiple container loading cost minimization problem [J]. European Journal of Operational Research, 2011, 14(3): 501–511.

[12] Chen C, LEE S, SHEN Q. An analytical model for the container loading problem [J]. European Journal of Operational Research, 1995, 80(1): 68–76.

[13] CHUNG F, GAREY M, JOHNSON D. On packing two-dimensional bins [J]. SIAM Journal on Algebraic Discrete Methods, 1982, 3(1): 66–76.

[14] CRAINIC T G, PERBOLI G, TADEI R. Extreme point-based heuristics for three-dimensional bin packing [J]. INFORMS Journal on Computing, 2008, 20(3): 368–384.

[15] CRAINIC T G, PERBOLI G, TADEI R. TS2PACK: A two-level tabu search for the three-dimensional bin packing problem [J]. European Journal of Operational Research, 2009, 195(3): 744–760.

[16] DAVIES A, BISCHOFF E. Weight distribution considerations in container loading [J]. European Journal of Operational Research, 1999, 114(3): 509–527.

[17] Boef E, Korst J, Martello S, et al. Erratum to the three-dimensional bin packing problem: robot-packable and orthogonal variants of packing problems [J]. Operations Research, 2005, 53(4): 735–736.

[18] DORIGO M, STUTZLE T. Ant colony optimization [M]. London: The MIT Press, 2004.

[19] DYCKHOFF H, FINKE U. Cutting and packing in production and distribution: a typology and bibliography [M]. Heidelberg: Physica-

Verlag, , 1992.

[20] ELEY M. Solving container loading problems by block arrangement [J]. European Journal of Operational Research, 2002, 141(2): 393–409.

[21] ELEY M. A bottleneck assignment approach to the multiple container loading problem [J]. OR Spectrum, 2003, 25(1): 45–60.

[22] FANSLAU T, BORTFELDT A. A tree search algorithm for solving the container loading problem [J]. INFORMS Journal on Computing, 2010, 22(2): 222–235.

[23] FAROE O, PISINGER D, ZACHARIASEN M,et al. Guided local search for the three-dimensional bin-packing problem [J]. INFORMS Journal on Computing, 2003, 15(3): 267–283.

[24] FASANO G. Cargo analytical integration in space engineering: a three-dimensional packing model [M]. London: Palgrave Macmillan, 1999.

[25] FEKETE S P, SCHEPERS J. On more-dimensional packing I: modeling [R]. Berlin : Department of Mathematics, Technical University Berlin, 1997.

[26] FEKETE S P, SCHEPERS J. On more-dimensional packing II: bounds [R]. Berlin : Department of Mathematics, Technical University Berlin, 1997.

[27] FEKETE S P, SCHEPERS J. A combinatorial characterization of higher-dimensional orthogonal packing [J] . Mathematics of Operations Research, 2004, 29(2): 353–368.

[28] FEKETE S P, SCHEPERS J. A general framework for bounds for higher-dimensional orthogonal packing problems [J]. Mathematical Methods of Operational Research, 2004, 60(2): 311–329.

[29] FEKETE S P, VAN DER， VEEN J C. PackLib2: an integrated library of multi - dimensional packing problems [J] . European Journal of Operational Research, 2007, 183(3): 1131–1135.

[30] FEKETE S P, SCHEPERS J, VAN DER VEEN J C. An exact algorithm for higher-dimensional orthogonal packing [J]. Operations Research, 2007, 55(3): 569–587.

[31] GEHRING H, BORTFELDT A. A genetic algorithm for solving the container loading problem [J]. International Transactions in Operational Research, 1997, 4(5–6): 401–418.

[32] GEHRING H, BORTFELDT A. A parallel genetic algorithm for solving the

container loading problem [J]. International Transactions in Operational Research, 2002, 9(4): 497–511.

[33] GEHRING H, MENSCHNER K, MEYER M. A computer-based heuristic for packing pooled shipment containers [J]. European Journal of Operational Research, 1990, 44(2): 277–288.

[34] GEORGE J, ROBINSON D. A heuristic for packing boxes into a container [J]. Computers & Operations Research, 1980, 7(3): 147–156.

[35] GILMORE P C, GOMORY R E. The theory and computation of knapsack functions [J]. Operations Research, 1966 , 14(6): 1045–1074.

[36] GLOVER F, KOCHENBERGER G. Handbook of metaheuristics [M]. Dordrecht: Kluwer Academic Publishers, 2003.

[37] GLOVER F, LAGUNA M. Tabu search [M]. Berlin: Springer, 1998.

[38] GOLDBERG D E. Genetic algorithms in search, optimization and machine learning [M]. Boston: Addison-Wesley Longman Publishing Co., Inc., 1989.

[39] HE C, ZHANG Y. Research of three-dimensional container-packing problems based on discrete particle swarm optimization algorithm: proceedings of 2009 International Conference on Test and Measurement, Hong Kong, December 5–6, 2009 [C]. New York: IEEE, 2010.

[40] HE K, HUANG W. An efficient placement heuristic for three-dimensional rectangular packing [J]. Computers & Operations Research, 2011, 38 (1): 227–233.

[41] HIFI M. Approximate algorithms for the container loading problem [J]. International Transactions in Operational Research, 2002, 9(6): 747–774.

[42] HIFI M. Exact algorithms for unconstrained three-dimensional cutting problems: a comparative study [J]. Computers & Operations Research, 2004, 31(5): 657–674.

[43] HIFI M, OUAFI R. Best-first search and dynamic programming methods for cutting problems: the cases of one or more stock plates [J]. Computers & Industrial Engineering, 1997, 32(1): 187–205.

[44] HIFI M, ZISSIMOPOULOS V. A recursive exact algorithm for weighted two-dimensional cutting [J]. European Journal of Operational Research, 1996, 91(3): 553–564.

[45] HOCHBAUM D S. Approximation algorithms for np-hard problems [M].

Boston: PWS Publishing Co., 1997.

[46] HUANG W, HE K. A caving degree approach for the single container loading problem [J]. European Journal of Operational Research, 2009, 196(1): 93–101.

[47] JANSEN K, SOLIS-OBA R. An asymptotic approximation algorithm for 3D-strip packing: proceedings of the Seventeenth Annual ACM-SIAM Symposium On Discrete Algorithm, New York, 2006 [C]. New York: ACM Press,2006.

[48] JIN Z, OHNO K, DU J. An efficient approach for the three-dimensional container packing problem with practical constraints [J]. Asia-Pacific Journal of Operational Research, 2004, 21(3): 279–295.

[49] JUNQUEIRA L, MORABITO R, SATO YAMASHITA D. Three-dimensional container loading models with cargo stability and load bearing constraints [J]. Computers & Operations Research, 2012, 39(1): 74–85.

[50] LEWIS R. A general-purpose hill-climbing method for order independent minimum grouping problems: a case study in graph colouring and bin packing [J]. Computers & Operations Research, 2009, 36(7): 2295–2310.

[51] LI K, CHENG K H. On three-dimensional packing [J]. SIAM Journal on Computing , 1990, 19(5):847–867.

[52] LI K, CHENG K H. Heuristic algorithms for on-line packing in three dimensions [J]. Journal of Algorithms, 1992, 13(4): 589–605.

[53] LIM A, RODRIGUES B, WANG Y. A multi-faced buildup algorithm for three-dimensional packing problems [J]. Omega, 2003, 31(6): 471–481.

[54] LODI A, MARTELLO S, VIGO D. Heuristic and metaheuristic approaches for a class of two-dimensional bin packing problems [J]. INFORMS Journal on Computing, 1999, 11(4): 345–357.

[55] LODI A, MARTELLO S, VIGO D. Heuristic algorithms for the three-dimensional bin packing problem [J]. European Journal of Operational Research, 2002, 141(2): 410–420.

[56] MACK D, BORTFELDT A, GEHRING H. A parallel hybrid local search algorithm for the container loading problem [J]. International Transactions in Operational Research, 2004, 11: 511–533.

[57] MARTELLO S, TOTH P. Knapsack problems: algorithms and computer implementations [M]. New York: John Wiley & Sons, Inc., 1990.

[58] MARTELLO S, PISINGER D, VIGO D. The three-dimensional bin packing problem [J]. Operations Research, 2000, 48(2): 256–267.

[59] MARTELLO S, PISINGER D, VIGO D, et al, . Algorithm 864: general and robot-packable variants of the three-dimensional bin packing problem [J]. ACM Transactions on Mathematical Software, 2007, 33(1).

[60] MIYAZAWA F, WAKABAYASHI Y. Parametric on-line algorithms for packing rectangles and boxes [J]. European Journal of Operational Research, 2003, 150(2): 281–292.

[61] MIYAZAWA F, WAKABAYASHI Y. Two-and three-dimensional parametric packing [J]. Computers & Operations Research, 2007, 34(9): 2589–2603.

[62] MIYAZAWA F, WAKABAYASHI Y. An algorithm for the three-dimensional packing problem with asymptotic performance analysis [J]. Algorithmica, 1997, 18: 122–144.

[63] MIYAZAWA F, WAKABAYASHI Y. Approximation algorithms for the orthogonal z-oriented three-dimensional packing problem [J]. SIAM Journal on Computing, 1999, 29(3): 1008–1029.

[64] MIYAZAWA F, WAKABAYASHI Y. Three-dimensional packings with rotations [J]. Computers & Operations Research, 2009, 36(10): 2801–2815.

[65] MORABITO R, ARENALEST M. An AND/OR-graph approach to the container loading problem [J]. International Transactions in Operational Research, 1994, 1(1): 59–73.

[66] MORABITO R, MORALES S. A simple and effective recursive procedure for the manufacturer's pallet loading problem [J]. Journal of the Operational Research Society, 1998, 49(8): 819–828.

[67] MOURA A, OLIVEIRA J. A GRASP Approach to the container-loading problem [J]. Intelligent Systems, 2005, 20(4): 50–57.

[68] NGOI B, WHYBREW K. A fast spatial representation method (applied to fixture design) [J]. The International Journal of Advanced Manufactu-ring Technology, 1993, 8(2): 71–77.

[69] NGOI B, TAY M, CHUA E. Applying spatial representation techniques to the container packing problem [J]. International Journal of Production Research, 1994, 32(1): 111–123.

[70] OLSSON A. Particle swarm optimization: theory, techniques and

applications [M]. New York: Nova Science Publishers, Incorporated, 2011.

[71] PADBERG M. Packing small boxes into a big box [J]. Mathematical Methods of Operations Research (ZOR), 2000, 52(1): 1–21.

[72] PARRENO F, ALVAREZ-VALDES R, OLIVEIRA J F,et al. Ahybrid GRASP/VND algorithm for two-and three-dimensional bin packing [J]. Annals of Operations Research,2008, 179(1): 203–220.

[73] PARRENO F, ALVAREZ-VALDES R, TAMARIT J M, et al. A maximal-space algorithm for the container loading problem [J]. INFORMS Journal on Computing, 2008, 20(3): 412–422.

[74] PISINGER D. A tree search algorithm for the container loading problem [J]. Ricerca Operativa, 1998, 83: 394–410.

[75] PISINGER D. Heuristics for the container loading problem [J]. European Journal of Operational Research, 2002, 141(2): 382–392.

[76] PORTMANN M C. An efficient algorithm for the container loading [J]. Methods of Operations Research, 1990, 64: 563–572.

[77] REN J, TIAN Y, SAWARAGI T. A tree search method for the container loading problem with shipment priority [J]. European Journal of Operational Research, 2011, 214(3): 526–535.

[78] SCHEITHAUER G. A three-dimensional bin packing algorithm [J]. Elektronische Informationsverarbeitung und kybernetik, 1991, 27: 263–271.

[79] SCHEITHAUER G. LP-based bounds for the container and multi-container loading problem [J]. International Transactions in Operational Research, 1999, 6(2): 199–213.

[80] SILVA J L D C, SOMA N Y, MACULAN N. A greedy search for the three-dimensional bin packing problem: the packing static stability case [J]. International Transactions in Operational Research, 2003, 10: 141–153.

[81] TAKAHARA S, MIYAMOTO S. An evolutionary approach for the multiple container loading problem: proceedings of the Fifth International Conference on Hybrid Intelligent Systems (HIS' 05), Rio de Janeiro, November 6–9, 2005 [C]. New York: IEEE, 2005.

[82] TALBI E G. Metaheuristics: from design to implementation [M]. USA: John Wiley & Sons, 2009.

[83] TERNO J, SCHEITHAUER G, RIEHME J, et al. An efficient approach for

the multi-pallet loading problem [J]. European Journal of Operational Research, 2000, 123: 372–381.

[84] VAN LAARHOVEN P, AARTS E. Simulated annealing: theory and applications [M]. German: Springer, 1987.

[85] VAZIRANI V. Approximation algorithms [M]. German: Springer, 2001.

[86] WASCHER G, HAUBNER H, SCHUMANN H. An improved typology of cutting and packing problems [J]. European Journal of Operational Research, 2007, 183(3): 1109–1130.

[87] WEI L, ZHU W, LIM A. A goal-driven prototype column generation strategy for the multiple container loading cost minimization problem [J]. European Journal of Operational Research, 2015, 241(1): 39–49. .

[88] XUE J, LAI K. Effective methods for a container packing operation [J]. Mathematical and Computer Modelling, 1997, 25(2): 75–84.

[89] ZHANG D, PENG Y, LEUNG S C. A heuristic block-loading algorithm based on multi-layer search for the container loading problem [J]. Computers & Operations Research, 2012, 39(10): 2267–2276.

[90] ZHU W, LIM A. A new iterative-doubling GreedyLook ahead algorithm for the single container loading problem [J]. European Journal of Operational Research, 2012, 222(3): 408–417.

[91] ZHU W, HUANG W, LIM A. A prototype column generation strategy for the multiple container loading problem [J]. European Journal of Operational Research, 2012, 223(1): 27–39.

[92] ZHU W, OON W C, LIM A, et al. The six elements to blockbuilding approaches for the single container loading problem [J]. Applied Intelligence, 2012, 37(3): 431–445.

Index

1.Approximation Algorithm

2.Beam Search

3.Binary Search

4.Block of Items

5.Block Selection

6.Calibrate Parameters

7.Combinatorial Optimization

8.Computational Experiment

9.Computational Results

10.Constructive Algorithm

11.Container

12.Container Cost

13.Container Loading Problem

14.Containment

15.Cutting and Packing Problem

16.Decision Support

17.Depalletizing

18.Exact Algorithm

19.Full Support

20.Generalized Container Loading Problem

21.Heuristic Method

22.Item

23.Item Preference

24.Item Value

25.Loading Constraints

26.Loading Plan

27.Mandatory Items

28.Mixed-Integer Linear Programming Model

29.Modeling Techniques

30.Multiple Container Loading Cost Minimization Problem

31.Multiple Container Loading Problem with Preference

32.No Overlap

33.NP-hard

34.Optional Items

35.Orientation Restriction

36.Orthogonal Placement

37.Pallet Storage Unit

38.Repalletizing

39.Residual Space

40.Set-Covering Model

41.Single Container Loading Problem

42.Single Container Mix-Loading Problem

43.Space Selection

44.Statistical Estimation

45.Test Instance

46.Three-Dimensional Bin Packing Problem

47.Three-Dimensional Variable-Sized Bin Packing Problem

48.Tree Search

49.Unit Shipping Cost

50.Volume Utilization